Visions
of a
Liberated Future

Visions
of a
Liberated Future
Black Arts
Movement Writings

Larry Neal

With Commentary by Amiri Baraka, Stanley Crouch,
Charles Fuller, and Jayne Cortez

Edited by Michael Schwartz

THUNDER'S
MOUTH
PRESS

NEW YORK

Published in the United States by Thunder's Mouth Press,
54 Greene Street, Suite 4S, New York, N.Y. 10013

First printing, 1989

Library of Congress Cataloging in Publication Data:

Neal, Larry, 1937–
       Visions of a liberated future : Black arts movement writing :
poetry and prose / by Larry Neal : with commentary by Amirl Baraka
. . . [et al.].
              p.   cm.
       ISBN 0-938410-78-4 : $19.95.—ISBN 0-938410-77-6 (pbk.) : $10.95
       1. Afro-Americans—Literary collections. 2. Afro-Americans—
—Intellectual life.   I. Title.
PS3564.E18V5   1989
818'5409—dc19   88-34653
                                                                     CIP

Grateful acknowledgement is made to the New York States Council on
the Arts and the National Endowment for the Arts for their assistance
in the publication of this work.

Grateful acknowledgement is made to Mrs. Evelyn Neal, Professor
Kimberly Benson, Jayne Cortez, Charles Fuller, Stanley Crouch, Amiri
Baraka, and Deirdre Bibby and Sule Greg Wilson of the Schomburg
Center for Research in Black Culture for their invaluable advice and
assistance in assembling this volume.

Some of these pieces have appeared in one version or another in the
following publications: *Callaloo, Liberator, Black World, The Black Scholar,
The Drama Review, Partisan Review, Black Review,* and *Essence*.

Text design by Terry McCabe.

Printed in the United States of America

Distributed by Consortium Book Sales and Distribution,
213 East 4th Street, St. Paul, MN. 55101

This book is dedicated to:

Larry's mother, Mrs. Maggie Neal,
  his brothers Melvin and Robby Neal,
   his son, Avatar Larry Neal,
    and the memory of Larry's brothers Joseph and Charles Neal,
    who died in 1988.

                                     —Mrs. Evelyn Neal

Contents

FOREWORD

The Wailer

I met Larry Neal in New York City as the Civil Rights Movement was turning into the Black Liberation Movement. That is, as the nonviolent struggle for democracy led by Dr. King was being superseded by the sector of the movement inspired by Malcolm X, who called for Self-Determination, Self-Respect, and Self-Defense.

I first met Larry as a political comrade, as part of the swelling numbers of young people raised watching Dr. King, beaten and assaulted, leading the masses in struggle against American *Apartheid*.

We came together, with a number of others, seeking to raise the level of black struggle to a more intense expression. We were young people who responded to the assassination of Patrice Lumumba by taking to the street, even invading the U.N. (way back when the U.S. controlled it) to show our opposition to U.S. imperialism.

(And it is important that we realize the pattern of their murders in U.S. imperialism's attempt to stop the international rise of Black Liberation and liberation movements in general. When the hot spot of the Black Liberation Movement was Africa, Lumumba, Sylvanus Olympio, Mondlane, Cabral were assassinated. When it moved to the U.S., Malcolm, King, Medgar Evers, Fred Hampton, and countless numbers of others. And now the hot spot is the Caribbean with the murders of Walter Rodney, Mikey Smith, Maurice Bishop, the mystery surrounding Bob Marley's death!)

We were young people on the move politically. No, we

would not turn the other cheek. No, we would not be passive in our resistance. Malcolm was our man, our voice, Self-Defense! We would fight.

Men like Rob Williams were heroes to us. Resisting and disarming the Klan. Threatening *Them!*

We would show these "crackers" (a term I learned from my Republican grandfather) that the days of their torture of black people, anywhere!, were long gone. We would fight. We would arm ourselves and fight.

Larry was there. Young, hip, talking black revolution. Clean as, and like the rest of us, arrogant as, the afternoon sun. Hot and brightly shining. Full of life, energy, and Black Fire!

I found out Larry was an artist, a poet, writer after our mutually expressed commitment to destroy white supremacy. It was the same with Askia Toure. We met fighting police while protesting Lumumba's murder. We found we both wrote poetry, afterward!

It was part of our commitment to the black revolutionary democratic struggle that we collaborated to create the Black Arts Repertory Theater School (BARTS) in Harlem. Both Larry and Askia were among the chief catalysts for that blazing and progressive, though short-lived, institution.

But the institution set a concrete example for the movement it was part of—the Black Arts Movement! The movement by young, black artists in the 60s to create an art, a literature that would fight for black people's liberation with as much intensity as Malcolm X our "Fire Prophet" and the rest of the enraged masses who took to the streets in Birmingham after the four little girls had been murdered by the Klan and FBI, or the ones who were dancing in the street in Harlem, Watts, Newark, Detroit.

We wanted an art that would actually reflect black life and its history and legacy of resistance and struggle!

We wanted an art that was as black as our music. A blues poetry (à la Langston and Sterling); a jazz poetry; a funky verse full of exploding antiracist weapons. A bebop and new music poetry that would scream and taunt and rhythm—attack the enemy into submission.

An art that would educate and unify black people in our attack on an anti-black racist America.

We wanted a *mass art,* an art that could "Monkey" out the libraries and "Boogaloo" down the street in tune with popular revolution. A poetry the people could sing as they beat Faubus and Wallace and Bull Connor to death!

What we wanted to create would be African American and Revolutionary. In fact it would be the real link to our history— part of the mainstream of black art through the century. However, we were not clear enough in our logical and spiritual antecedents: e.g., if we had only read Langston's "The Negro Artist and the Racial Mountain" in high school, many of the twists and turns of our quest for self-understanding would have been short cut. The movement at still higher levels.

Larry was an innovator in that regard. He was a spiritual leader of that movement. One of the hot lipped hip bebop poetry warriors trying to take the language someplace else, just as King and Malcolm were trying to take the whole society someplace else. Just as Jesse is trying to take the place into space today!

I felt almost immediately a close connection with Larry. We were very much alike in a lot of ways. Artists who wanted to make revolution. Revolutionary intellectuals. Trying to bring our bebop love into the streets of rebellion.

And throughout the existence of the BARTS Larry was a constant source of intelligence and inspiration. We demanded a lot from ourselves, but finally did not have the science at our disposal to transform rebellion into revolution. Yet the direction, the intention; e.g., the need for black institutions that would carry and reinterpret the revolutionary democratic black imperative in the U.S. Carry and sustain it, create it, generation after generation at yet higher levels. The need for them still exists. Even worse now than in the 60s when the spontaneous fire of the people overturned reaction and backwardness. Yet nothing can be accomplished just by spontaneous struggle. There must be scientific ideology and scientific organization. The BARTS is where we first learned that, in quite painful fashion. In fact when I left Harlem, under duress of ignorance and the FBI, Larry was shot for attempting to maintain revolutionary integrity in the face of provocateurs and scum.

But what is so important is that because our words were words created by revolutionary passion, the inspiration, the focus, the skills we had as artists expanded by our very commitment to revolution. Larry Neal and Askia Toure were my models in the middle 60s for Black Art. We wanted the oral tradition in our work, we wanted the sound, the pumping rhythm of black music. The signifying drawl of blues. Larry incorporated it all into his work. High intelligence, revolutionary commitment, and great skill. Which is why it infuriates me when I hear young economist artists (as Lenin termed them), more interested in careerism and getoverism than Black Liberation, try to put down the artists of the 60s for lack of skill. What dismally brainwashed opportunistic vulture feces.

As if it took no skill to move the people, to have the black masses wailing our love songs to Self-Determination, Self-Respect and Self-Defense, as they struggled to change the world. It took much more skill, it takes much more skill, to move the people than it does simply to stand in the bossman's payline to get a gig as occasionally mentioned whore in the national lie. Which is where a lot of folks have gone, in collaborative celebration of the steady deadly move to fascism and nuclear war set forth as examples of human dignity by the fascist-minded Ronald Reagan and his white supremacy *über alles* regime!

Art does not have to be philosophically and ideologically reactionary. It is possible (and necessary) to struggle for human development, for liberation and social transformation in art. We do not have to create *Birth of a Nation* or the *Cantos* to be great artists. We do not have to support fascists or white supremacy to be "immortal." Only the bourgeoisie, the ignorant, or servants of the above think this. Larry did not think it.

Ghost Poem # 1

You would never shoot smack
or lay in one of these Harlem
doorways pissing on yourself
that is not your way
not the
way of Alabama boys groomed slick
for these wicked cities momma
warned us of

You were always swifter than that:
the fast money was the Murphy game
or the main supply before the cutting—
so now you lean with the shadows
(at the dark end of Turk's bar)
aware that the hitman is on your ass

You know that there is something inevitable
about it
You know that he will come
as sure as shit
snorting blow for courage
and he will burn you at the peak of your peacocking
glory
And when momma gets the news
she will shudder over the evening meal
and moan: "Is that my Junie Boy runnin
with that fast crowd?"

(Larry Neal)

During the BARTS period Larry was also one of the featured writers in *Liberator* magazine, published by Dan Watts, which was one of the most progressive periodicals of the period. Larry's literary criticism, his political commentary were incisive signal flags of our movement. Teaching us and goading us and giving us hope and information. And during his time, Larry was not only poet and essayist, he wrote drama and screenplays. One of our most important collaborations was the anthology *Black Fire* (now out of print), which collected the key black artists of the period, young and fire hot, to show the way the Black Arts Movement spelled out. But obviously, in this present period, such an anthology is economically banned as too far out, too hot, too "racist," man them niggers were crazy, et cetera. But the book set the tone and direction for the literary revolution in progress. And Larry's hand was key in the shaping of that work.

We also collaborated later on the magazine *Cricket*, a publication devoted to African-American music (wish we had it today). Larry was one of the editors, along with A. B. Spellman and myself. It had only three issues, but they were significant in that for the first time, black people were defining their art, their aesthetic, their social aesthetic, their social and aesthetic ideology, not someone else. Both these publications were black nationalist. As were Larry and myself and countless others during the period. Many of us have moved to the left since that period. And some of our metaphysics and crass cultural nationalism is embarrassing even to us, but the essence of the work was resistance to imperialism, resistance to white supremacy, even in its flawed form. Our Hearts were Good! Good & Black!

Such institutions as the BARTS and *Cricket,* and publishing African-American artists, is still critical for us, especially in a backward period such as this. But our lack of institutions itself contributes to the backwardness!

You see our traditions, which we are often late to understand, if we persevere as intellectuals or continue them naturally and spontaneously as part of the mass cultures and intelligence—our traditions, the politics, art, culture of the African-American people, have always been, in the main, *democratic* and because of this—in the context of chattel slavery, reaction, white supremacy, racism, national oppression—our traditions are *revolutionary*.

We have yet to experience bourgeois democracy. It still amazes me to hear Americans talk about this place, because, to paraphrase Langston, "America never was America/to me."

That revolutionary democratic (yet highly elegant tradition) was what Larry Neal carried and upheld.

Shit, to look at Larry, with his ultra-hip. Philadelphia self, was to look at the *art* of being oneself. His very sartorial splendor was a *statement,* both obvious and profound. One that alto artist Arthur Blythe confirms as *In the Tradition!*

Too many black intellectuals forfeit this tradition brainwashed and humiliated their negro *training* which they mistake as education. We get degrees in other, from other, to be always very other than ourselves or somebody our grandmama would *recognize* as righteous carriers of the spirit which animated those "Black and Unknown Bards."

Larry came at a period of rising political intensity, struggle and consciousness. He passed it on, like the black baton of our history to any who knew him or was moved or influenced by him—by anyone who could read.

Because Larry Neal, when all the shouting and lying is done, perhaps when there really is a *free world* (contrary to white racist bully imperialism's definition of that nonexistent paradigm), Larry will emerge as one of the truly *wonderful* artists of our age. A great poet, visionary essayist, and important dramatist. Even as he is known *now* by those of us sufficiently disconnected from the aesthetic of dying murderers to appreciate truth made beautiful!

Poppa Stoppa Speaks from His Grave

Remember me baby in my best light,
lovely hip style and all;
all laid out in my green velour
stashing on corners
in my boxcar coat—
so sure of myself, too cool for words,
and running down a beautiful game.

It would be super righteous
if you would think of me that way sometimes;
and since it can't be that way,
just the thought of you digging on me that way
would be hip and lovely even from here.

Yeah, you got a sweet body, baby,
but out this way, I won't be needing it;
but remember me and think of me
that way sometimes.

But don't make it no big thing though;
don't jump jive and blow your real romance.
but in a word, while you high-steppin and finger-poppin
tell your lovin' man that I was a bad
motherfucker till the Butcher cut me down.

(Larry Neal)

Now three years after Larry's tragic premature death, this conference is important, and it is made even more so by its carrying his name. And by so doing, hopefully, helping to spread and revive the power and relevance of Larry's art and political message.

Today, we are in a reactionary period similar to the 1880s when after the Civil War and the abortive attempt at Reconstruction, black people were betrayed by almost every segment of the American population and thrown down into the neo-slavery of sharecropping and separate but evil American Apartheid.

The period Larry Neal and I came to consciousness in was a highly political, highly progressive period. Twenty years later, after the multiple assassinations of our leaders, the Cointelpro wrecking of our movement, we see the very people that murdered Malcolm, Martin (and for that matter John and Robert Kennedy) sitting in the White House trying to murder the world!!

We see people who used to call themselves revolutionaries trying to cleave their way into the Mormon church, or writing barbecue cookbooks, or hidden away somewhere trying to be cool in the face of monsters.

This is not in the spirit of Larry Neal, nor is it in the great tradition of the African-American people.

It is significant that this conference, the second, should come now when there is some sign of a reawakening and reconstruction of the movement. Jesse Jackson's candidacy is straight ahead in the tradition of resistance and struggle that has characterized the African-American spirit. People want to know why Jesse Jackson speaks in rhymes. Black leaders have to be poets, otherwise the people wouldn't listen! Because the mainstream of black poetry has always touched and been touched by that revolutionary democratic spirit and was therefore always close to the people and close to the movement. This is what Larry Neal's art is all about. It is like the mass line that Mao Zedong talks about, "From the people to the people." We use our skill and the people's fire.

We opposed the dead literature of the dying criminal imperialist culture because that literature is a method of recruiting us into the empire of exploitation and oppression, or madness and irrelevance.

Sound, Light, Heat, Spirit, Rhythm, Movement, Transformation—not criminal boredom and irrelevance, not support of what cannot be supported.

Larry's work is universal because the human spirit struggling for revelation/revolution is seen across the world. The greatest artists of any culture are those upholding the upward motion of the human spirit—the will of the majority to transform the world and itself in that world.

The spirit Larry Neal's work will contain forever is the spirit of the world constantly being reborn, of renaissance and new life. It is a spirit that will motivate the billions of us until the planet explodes.

The many tasks and treks and acts Larry speaks of, will speak of, still need to be accomplished. The raising of consciousness, opposition to reaction, need for institutions and a revolutionary art are still priorities needing to be brought into reality.

If we do not build revolutionary institutions, for instance, Larry Neal's works might disappear or become obscure. They will not be honored by our enemies, just as freedom ain't never been free.

Larry is an example for us. Read his work. Heed his example and imperatives. Understand why he was so hip. It is all critical and necessary. As we pass the baton from generation to generation. We see our cultural workers falling on all sides. Suicided by imperialism. Larry Neal, dead of a heart attack, age 43.

It means we have not created what we need to preserve ourselves and kill our enemies. It means we are still in the middle passage. Let us honor our fallen comrade and bother Larry Neal, by honoring his work and bringing into reality its demanding vision!!!

Wailers

For Larry Neal and Bob Marley

Wailers we are
We are Wailers. Dont get scared.
Nothing happening but out and way out.
Nothing happening but the positive. (Unless you are the negative.)
    Wailers.
We wailers. Yeh, wail. Yeh, wailers.
We wail, we wail.

We

We could dig Melville on his ship
confronting the huge white mad beast
speeding death cross the sea to we.
But we whalers. We can kill whales.
We could get on top of a whale
and wail. Wailers. Undersea defense hot folk
Blue babies humming when we arrive. Boogie ladies strumming our
black violet souls. Rag daddies come from the land of never say die.
Reggae workers bringing the funk to the people of I. We wailers
alright.

Hail to you Bob, man! We will ask your question all our lives.
Could You Be Loved? I and I understand. We see the world
Eyes and eyes say Yes to transformation. Wailers. Aye, Wailers.
Subterranean night color Magis, working inside the soul of
    the world.
Wailers. Eyes seeing the world's being

Hey, Bob, Wail on rock on Jah come into us as real vision and action
Hey, Larry, Wail on, with Lester and the Porkpie, wailing us energy
for truth. We Wailers is all, and on past that to say, wailing for all
we worth. Rhythm folks obsessed with stroking what is with our
sound purchase.

Call Me Thelonius, in my crowded Wail Vessel, I hold the keys
    to the
funk kingdom. Lie on me if you want to, tell folks its yours
But for real wailing not tale telling, the sensitive know who the
    Waile
Be We. Be We. We Wailers. Blue Blowers. The Real Rhythm Kings.
We sing philosophy. Hambone precise findings. Image Masters of the
syncopated. Wailers & Drummers.
                    Wailers & Trumpet stars.
                    Wailers & Box cookers.
                    Wailers & sax flyers.
                    Wailers & bass thumpers.
                    Wailers and Hey, wail, wail. We Wailers!
                    Trombone benders. Magic singers.
                    Ellingtonians.
The only Tranes faster than rocket ships. Shit.
Cut a rocket in our pocket and put a chord on the wall of the wind.
Wailers. Can you dig Wailing?

Call Me Bud Powell. You wanna imitate this?
Listen. Spree dee deet sprree deee whee spredeee shee deee

My calling card. The dialectic of silence.
The Sound approach.
Life one day will be filled even further with we numbers we song
But primitive place now, we wailing be kept underground.

But keep it in mind. Call me something Dukish. Something sassy.
Call me by my real name. When the world change
We wailing be in it, help make it, for real time.

Call Me. I'll call you. We call We.
Say, Hey Wailers. Hey, Wailers.
Hey hey hey, Wailers. Wail On!

—AMIRI BARAKA*
Second Annual Larry Neal Writers' Conference
Washington, D.C. 1983

*Elsewhere in this volume, Amiri Baraka is also referred to as Imamu Amiri Baraka and as LeRoi Jones.

Essays

INTRODUCTION

The Incomplete Turn of Larry Neal

An early death is most tragic when someone fully capable of executing a personal plan is snuffed out before bringing it off. Now that Larry Neal has been dead almost ten years, I understand that fact much better, especially after reading his essays collected in this volume. Beyond the congenital misfortune of Larry Neal's heart attack, there is another grim fact: death can deem the weight of a man's work a failure. This is not the same as ones success as a person—the sensitivity, affection, wit, passion, intellectual curiosity, and challenge someone can so consistently bring to social and intimate friendships that the loss of a particular presence is deeply mourned. Though Larry Neal had those qualities, and exhibits them in the best of the work included here, he never really achieved what he was after *in literary terms*. He was just shaking off the conventions of black nationalist thought that had driven his intellect to the canvas, was in the process of taking a few rounds, and had a grand strategy for what he was going to do all the way through the fifteenth when he left the ring feet first.

In a sense, Larry was not only a product but a victim of the anger, despair, and frustration that began to dominate the thought of many younger black artists and writers in the middle sixties as the tactics and achievements of the civil rights movement were spurned in favor of ideas coming from Malcolm X and Frantz Fanon. When those ideas were not racist, they were couched in an ethnic version of Marxist revolution that embraced Third World liberation movements and applauded what was then considered the inevitable fall of Western capital-

3

ist democracies. Borrowing from Mao Zedong's Yan'an speech on literature and art, those who thought themselves at the forefront of a black cultural revolution perceived creation as an assault weapon and an affirmation of the virtues of the common people.

In a number of these essays, one encounters the philosophical attacks on the systems of the Western world, romantic celebrations of African purity, denunciations of the purported Uncle Toms who didn't embrace separatist and violent "solutions" to the American race problem, and the demand that all serious younger black artists commit themselves to a particular vision of political change. Such writing is now more important in terms of its relationship to the thought processes that underlay the work of a generation that produced nothing close to a masterpiece, that failed, as all propaganda—however well intentioned—inevitably fails. We learn little about the human soul from most of that writing: it exists more as evidence of a peculiar aspect of social history than any kind of aesthetic achievement.

But Larry Neal is important because he was one of the first who had been taken in by the self-segregation of black nationalist thinking to realize how little it had to offer and how easily it prepared the way for demagogues. Over the last decade of his life, Larry became more and more concerned with writing a body of work that could take its place on the shelf with the intellectual champions of this and any previous time—wherever they might come from, regardless of their color or class or religion. He was focusing on what Ornette Coleman calls "the human reason," which is the mysterious area all truly ambitious writers must address.

To address that inevitable body of mystery, Larry had to slowly, even painfully, tear himself free of the presumptions that were once thought bold and insightful but were actually manifestations of intellectual sleeping sickness. Even though still caught in the nationalist vision of the world, Larry is moving away from it in "My Lord He Calls Me by the Thunder" (p. 118), where he questions the outright rejection of the black Christian church, which was under attack from Negro Muslims on one hand and Marxists on the other. In "The Ethos of the Blues" (p. 107), he rejects the limited vision of Ron

Karenga, whose cultural nationalism never allowed for the appreciation of art that couldn't be utilized as part of a mishmash of racism and saber rattling. "Uncle Rufus Raps on the Squared Circle" (p. 97) tips its hat to Langston Hughes's Simple stories but contains a startling moment when the listener within the essay suddenly appears inside an example of the subject being explained by Uncle Rufus. Larry's ability to see through Baldwin's self-pitying Niagara of tears, and to recognize the need for a more comprehensive use of Afro-American culture in fiction, is another example of the hairpin turn he was making.

The best essay included here "Ralph Ellison's Zoot Suit" (p. 30) shows were he was going and finds him rejecting the impositions of propagandist rhetoric on serious literary work. Larry did such a good job of assessing the issues raised by *Invisible Man* and the responses to it that one can quite clearly see where he intended to go and how much he admired Ellison's refusal to be used by placard carriers. It was a statement of intellectual rebirth and a declaration of war against simplistic thinking.

That Larry Neal was never able to write another essay as good has less to do with his talent than the time he was allowed by the riddling whirlpool of human fate. Personal problems and a job in Washington, D.C. had taken up a lot of his time, but he was working to prepare himself for the next stage of his development when he died. Even though I knew him well and talked with him often, I have no idea what he would have done once he got down to the business he intended to take care of, part of which was shaping a more comprehensive aesthetic vision in light of all that had failed, in literary terms, by adhering to the doctrines of ethnic propaganda. But since he was coming to better understand the importance of the Afro-American culture that so many black nationalists and would-be revolutionaries had such contempt for, I have no trouble imagining that he would have become much more the writer his own ambitions demanded. That he was never able to become that writer is a tragedy of no small proportion, given the astonishing amount of trash that has been written on the subject of Negro American life since his death. Even so, there is much inspiration to be drawn from the fact that Larry Neal, when it was far from popular in his circle, was proudly starting to celebrate the bittersweet complexity of his identity as an American.

—STANLEY CROUCH

February 1, 1989

And Shine Swam On

Just then the Captain said, "Shine, Shine, save poor me,
I'll give you more money than a nigger ever see."
Shine said to the Captain: "Money is good on land and on
    sea,
but the money on land is the money for me."
And Shine swam on . . .
Then the Captain's lily white daughter come up on deck,
She had her hands on her pussy and her dress around her
    neck.
She says, "Shine, Shine, save poor me,
I'll give you more pussy than a nigger ever see."
Shine, he say, "There's pussy on land and pussy on sea,
but the pussy on land is the pussy for me."
And Shine swam on.

The quote is taken from an urban "toast" called "The *Titanic*."
It is part of the private mythology of black America. Its symbolism is direct and profound. Shine is US. We have been below-
deck stoking the ship's furnaces. Now the ship is sinking, but
where will we swim? This is the question that the "New
Breed," which James Brown sings about, asks.

"We don't have all of the answers, but have attempted,
through the artistic and political work presented here, to confront our problems from what must be called a radical perspective. Therefore, most of the book can be read as if it were a
critical reexamination of Western political, social and artistic
values. It can be read also as a rejection of anything that we
feel is detrimental to our people. And it is almost axiomatic

7

that most of what the West considers important endangers the more humane world we feel ours should be.

We have been, for the most part, talking about contemporary realities. We have not been talking about a return to some glorious African past. But we recognize the past—the total past. Many of us refuse to accept a truncated Negro history which cuts us off completely from our African ancestry. To do so is to accept the very racist assumptions which we abhor. Rather, we want to comprehend history totally, and understand the manifold ways in which contemporary problems are affected by it.

There is a tension within black America. And it has its roots in the general history of the race. The manner in which we see this history determines how we act. How should we see this history? What should we feel about it? This is important to know because the sense of how that history should be felt is what either unites or separates us.

For, how the thing is felt helps to determine how it is played. For example, the 1966 uprising in Watts is a case of feeling one's history in a particular way, and then acting it out in the most immediate manner possible. The emotions of the crowd have always played an integral role in the making of history.

Again, what separates a Malcolm X from a Roy Wilkins is a profound difference in what each believes the history of America to be. Finally, the success of one leader over another depends upon which one best understands and expresses the emotional realities of a given historical epoch. Hence, we feel a Malcolm in a way that a Roy Wilkins, a King, and a Whitney Young can never be felt. Because a Malcolm, finally, interprets the emotional history of his people better than the others.

There is a tension throughout our communities. The ghosts of that tension are Nat Turner, Martin Delany, Booker T. Washington, Frederick Douglass, Malcolm X, Garvey, [James] Monroe Trotter, DuBois, Fanon, and a whole panoply of mythical heroes from Brer Rabbit to Shine. These ghosts have left us with some very heavy questions about the realities of life for black people in America.

The movement is now faced with a serious crisis. It has postulated a theory of Black Power; and that is good. But it has failed to evolve a workable ideology. That is, a workable concept—perhaps Black Power is it—which can encompass many of the diverse ideological tendencies existent in the black community. This concept would have to allow for separatists and revolutionaries; and it would have to take into consideration the realities of contemporary American power, both here and abroad. The militant wing of the movement has begun to deny the patriotic assumptions of the white and negro establishment, but it has not supported that denial with a consistent theory of social change, one that must be rooted in the history of African-Americans.

Currently, there is a general lack of clarity about how to proceed. This lack of clarity is historical and is involved with what DuBois called the "double consciousness":

> this sense of always looking at one's self through the eyes of others, of measuring one's soul by the tape of a world that looks on in amused contempt and pity. One ever feels his twoness—an American, a Negro—two souls, two thoughts, two unreconciled strivings; two warring ideals in one dark body, whose dogged strength alone keeps it from being torn asunder.
> The history of the American Negro is the history of this strife—this longing to attain self-conscious manhood, to merge his double-self into a better and truer self. . . .

This statement is from *The Souls of Black Folk*, which was published in 1897. The double consciousness still exists, was even in existence prior to 1897.

Nat Turner, Denmark Vesey, and Gabriel Prosser attempted to destroy this double consciousness in bloody revolt.

In 1852, a black physician, Martin Delany, published a book entitled *The Destiny of the Colored Peoples*. Delany advocated repatriation—return to the Motherland (Africa). He believed that the United States would never fully grant black people freedom; and never would there be anything like "equal status with the white man."

Frederick Douglass, and many of the abolitionists, strongly believed in the "promise of America." But the double consciousness and its resulting tension still exist. How else can we explain the existence of these same ideas in contemporary America? Why was Garvey so popular? Why is it that in a community like Harlem one finds a distinctly nationalistic element which is growing yearly, according to a recent article in the *New York Times*? And it is a contemporary nationalism, existing in varying degrees of sophistication; but all of its tendencies, from the Revolutionary Action Movement (RAM) to the African Nationalist Pioneer Movement, are focused on questions not fully resolved by the established Negro leadership— questions which that leadership, at this stage of its development, is incapable of answering.

Therefore, the rebirth of the concept of Black Power opens old wounds. For the conflict between Booker T. Washington, and W. E. B. DuBois was essentially over the question of power, over the relationship of that power to the status of black America. The focus of the conflict between Washington and DuBois was education: What was the best means of educating black people? Should it be primarily university education, as advocated by DuBois; or one rooted in what Washington called "craft skills"? Since education functions in a society to enforce certain values, both men found it impossible to confine discussion simply to the nature of black education. It became a political question. It is a political question. Therefore, what was essentially being debated was the political status of over ten million people of African descent who, against their wills, were forced to eke out an existence in the United States.

Queen Mother Moore once pointed out that black people were never collectively given a chance to decide whether they wanted to be American citizens or not. After the Civil War, for example, there was no plebiscite putting the question of American citizenship to a vote. Therefore, implicit in the turn-of-the-century controversy between Washington and DuBois is the idea that black people are a nation—a separate nation apart from white America. Around 1897, the idea was more a part of Washington's thinking than DuBois's; but it was to haunt DuBois until the day he died (in Ghana).

The educational ideas of both Washington and DuBois were doomed to failure. Both ideas, within the context of American values, were merely the extension of another kind of oppression. Only, now it was an oppression of the spirit. Within the context of a racist America, both were advocating a "colonialized" education; that is, an education equivalent to the kind the native receives, in Africa and Asia, under the imperialists. The fundamental role of education in a racist society would have to be to "keep the niggers in their place."

All of the Negro colleges in this country were, and are even now, controlled by white money—white power. DuBois recognized this after he was dismissed from Atlanta University. In 1934, he further proceeded to advocate the establishment of independent "segregated" institutions and the development of the black community as a separate entity. The advocacy of such ideas led to a break with the NAACP, which was committed to a policy of total integration into American society. Here, then, is the tension, the ambiguity between integration and segregation, occurring in the highest ranks of a well-established middle-class organization. Hence in 1934, DuBois had not really advanced, at least not in terms of the ideas postulated above, but was merely picking up the threads of arguments put forth by Washington and Marcus Garvey. And the double consciousness dominated his entire professional life.

He had been everything that was demanded of him: scholar, poet, politician, nationalist, integrationist, and finally, in old age, a Communist. His had been a life full of controversy. He knew much about human nature, especially that of his people, but he did not understand Garvey—Garvey—who was merely his own double-consciousness theory personified in a very dynamic and forceful manner. Garvey was, in fact, attempting the destruction of that very tension which had plagued all of DuBois's professional career.

It involved knowing and deciding who and what we are. Had Garvey an organizational apparatus equivalent to the NAACP's, the entire history of the world might have been different. For Garvey was more emotionally cohesive than DuBois, and not as intellectually fragmented. DuBois, for all of his commitment, was a somewhat stuffy intellectual with middle-class hang-ups, for which Garvey constantly attacked him. The people to whom Garvey appealed could never have understood DuBois. But Garvey understood them, and the life-force within him was very fundamental to them. The NAACP has never had

the kind of fervent appeal that the Garvey movement had. It
has rarely understood the tension within the black masses. To
them, Garvey was a fanatic. But are these the words of a
fanatic, or of a lover?

> The NAACP wants all to become white by amalga-
> mation, but they are not honest enough to come out
> with the truth. To be a Negro is no disgrace, but an
> honor, and we of the UNIA [United Negro Improve-
> ment Association] do not want to become white. . . .
> We are proud and honorable. We love our race and
> respect and adore our mothers.

And, in a letter to his followers from prison:

> My months of forcible removal from among you,
> being imprisoned as a punishment for advocating the
> cause of our real emancipation, have not left me
> hopeless or despondent; but to the contrary, I see a
> great ray of light and the bursting of a mighty politi-
> cal cloud which will bring you complete freedom. . . .
> We have gradually won our way back into the
> confidence of the God of Africa, and He shall speak
> with a voice of thunder, that shall shake the pillars of
> a corrupt and unjust world, and once more restore
> Ethiopia to her ancient glory. . . .
> Hold fast to the Faith. Desert not the ranks, but as
> brave soldiers march on to victory. I am happy, and
> shall remain so, as long as you keep the flag flying.

So, in 1940, Garvey died. He died in London, an exile. He
was a proud man whose real fault was not lack of intense
feeling and conviction, but an inability to tailor his nationalism
to the realities of the American context. And also he was a
threat to Europe's colonial designs in Africa, a much greater
threat than the Pan-African conferences DuBois used to organize. Garvey wanted a nation for his people. That would have
meant the destruction of British, French, and Portuguese imperialism in Africa. And since it was a movement directed by
blacks here in this country, it would also have internally chal-
lenged American imperialism as it existed at that time.

But Garvey was no Theodor Herzl or Chaim Weizmann,[1] with their kind of skills and resources behind him. Had he been, he might have brought a nation into existence. But neither he nor his people had those kinds of resources, and, worse, the black bourgeoisie of the period did not understand him with the same intensity as the masses.

In 1940, the year Garvey died, Malcolm Little was fifteen years old. He caught a bus from Lansing, Michigan, and went to Boston to live with his sister, Ella Collins, who is now head of the organization Malcolm started when he broke with the Nation of Islam. It is probably the most important bus ride in history.

Malcolm X, whose father had been a Garveyite, was destined to confront the double consciousness of black America. But his confrontation would be a modern one, rooted in the teachings of the Nation of Islam and in the realities of contemporary politics. That is to say, his ideas would be a synthesis of black nationalism's essential truths as derived from Martin Delany, DuBois, Garvey, the Honorable Elijah Muhammad, Fanon, and Richard Wright. And his speech would be marked by a particular cadence, a kind of "hip" understanding of the world. It was the truth as only the oppressed, and those whose lives have somehow been "outside of history," could know it.

Civil rights and brotherhood were in vogue when Malcolm started "blowing"—started telling the truth in a manner only a deaf man would ignore. And many of us were deaf, or if not, in a deep sleep. He shot holes through the civil rights movement that was the new "in" for the white liberals. James Baldwin was also "in," pleading for a new morality to people who saw him as another form of entertainment. And there were sit-ins, pray-ins, sleep-ins, nonviolence, and the March on Washington. And the voice of Malcolm cut through it all, stripping away the sham and the lies. He was the conscience of black America, setting out, like a warrior, to destroy the double consciousness. He did not eschew dialogue. He attempted, instead, to make it more meaningful by infusing some truth into it. For this reason, it was both painful and beautiful to listen to him.

Malcolm covered everything—nationhood, manhood, the family, brotherhood, history, and the Third World revolution. Yet it always seemed to me that he was talking about a revolution of the psyche, about how we should see ourselves in the world.

But, just as suddenly as he was thrust among us—he was gone. Gone, just as black America was starting to understand what he was talking about. And those who killed him did so for just that reason. For Malcolm wanted to make real the internationalism of Garvey and DuBois. Our problem had ceased to be one of civil rights, he argued, but is, instead, one of human rights. As such—he extended the argument—it belongs in an international context. Like Garvey and DuBois before him, he linked the general oppression of black America to that of the Third World. Further, he strongly advocated unity with that world, something few civil rights leaders have dared to do.

Hence, what has come to be known as Black Power must be seen in terms of the ideas and persons that preceded it. Black Power is, in fact, a synthesis of all of the nationalistic ideas embedded within the double consciousness of black America. But it has no one specific meaning. It is rather a kind of feeling—a kind of emotional response to one's history. The theoreticians among us can break down its components. However, that will not be enough, for like all good theories, it can ultimately be defined only in action—in movement. Essentially, this is what the "New Breed" is doing—defining itself through actions, be they artistic or political.

We have attempted through these historical judgments to examine the idea of nationhood, the idea, real or fanciful, that black people comprise a separate national entity within the dominant white culture. This sense of being separate, especially within a racist society with so-called democratic ideas, has created a particular tension within the psychology of black America. We are saying, further, that this sense of the "separate" moves through much of today's black literature.

There is also a concomitant sense of being at "war." Max Stanford explains that this sense began the minute the first slaves were snatched from their lands. These two tensions, "separation" and "war," are pressing historical realities; both are leading to a literature of Armageddon.

We must face these ideas in all of their dimensions. In some cases, the literature speaks to the tension within, say, the family; or it deals with the nature of black manhood. At other times, especially in something like Jimmy Garrett's play *We Own the Night*, the "war" seems directed against an unseen white enemy; it is, in fact, an attack on the Uncle Tomism of the older generation.

The tension, or double consciousness, is most often resolved in violence, simply because the nature of our existence in America has been one of violence. In some cases, the tension resolves in recognizing the the beauty and love within black America itself. No, not a new "Negritude," but a profound sense of a unique and beautiful culture; and a sense that there are many spiritual areas to explore within this culture. This is a kind of separation but there is no tension about it. There is a kind of peace in the separation. This peace may be threatened by the realities of the beast world; yet, it is lived as fully as life can be lived. This sense of a haven in blackness is found most often in the poetry selections.

But history weighs down on all of this literature. Every black writer in America has had to react to this history, either to make peace with it, or make war with it. It cannot be ignored. Every black writer has chosen a particular stance toward it. He or she may tell you that, for them, it was never a problem. But they will be liars.

Most contemporary black writing of the last few years, the literature of the young, has been aimed at the destruction of the double consciousness. It has been aimed at consolidating the African-American personality. And it has not been essentially a literature of protest. It has, instead, turned its attention inward to the internal problems of the group. The problem of living in a racist society, therefore, is something that lurks on the immediate horizon, but which cannot be dealt with until certain political, social, and spiritual truths are understood by the oppressed themselves—inwardly understood.

It is a literature primarily directed at the consciences of black people. And, in that sense, it is a literature that is somewhat more mature than that which preceded it. The white world—the West—is seen now as a dying creature, totally bereft of spirituality. This being the case, the only hope is for some kind of psychic withdrawal from its values and assumptions. Not just America, but most of the noncolored world had been in the process of destroying the spiritual roots of mankind, while not substituting anything meaningful for this destruction.

Therefore, many see the enslavement of the Third World as an enslavement of the spirit. Marxists carefully analyze the material reasons for this kind of oppression, but it takes a Fanon to illustrate the spiritual malaise in back of this enslavement. I tend to feel that the answer lies outside of historical materialism. It is rooted in how man sees himself in the spiritual sense, in what he construes existence to mean. Most Western philosophical orientations have taken the force of meaning out of existence.

Why this has happened is not really known, at least not in any sense that is final. We do know that the Western mind construes reality differently from that of the rest of the world. Or, should I say, feels reality differently? Western mythological configurations are even vastly different from other configurations. Such configurations lead to the postulation of certain ideas of what art is, of what life is.

Let us take, for example, the disorientation one experiences when one sees a piece of African sculpture in a Madison Avenue art gallery. Ask yourself: What is it doing there? In Africa, the piece had ritual significance. It was a spiritual affirmation of the connection between man and his ancestors, and it implied a particular kind of ontology—a particular sense of being. However, when you see it in that gallery, you must recognize that no African artist desired that it be placed there. Rather, it was stolen by force and placed there. And the mind that stole it was of a different nature from the mind that made it.

In the gallery or the salon, it is merely an objet d'art, but for your ancestors, it was a bridge between them and the spirit, a bridge between you and your soul in the progression of a spiritual lineage. It was art, merely incidentally, for it was essentially functional in its natural setting. The same goes for music, song, dance, the folktale, and dress. All of these things were coalesced, with form and function unified. All of these were an evocation of the spirit, which included an affirmation of daily life and the necessity of living life with honor.

The degree to which the artists among us understand some of these things is the degree to which we shall fashion a total art form that speaks primarily to the needs of our people. The temptation offered by Western society is to turn from these essential truths and merge with the oppressor for solace. This temptation demands, not merely integration of the flesh, but also integration of the spirit. And there are few of us for whom this would not have dire consequences. Further, the tension, the double-consciousness of which we have already spoken, cannot be resolved in so easy a manner, especially when, within the context of the racist society, the merger has little chance of being a healthy one.

In an essay entitled "Blue Print for Negro Writing," Richard Wright attempted to define all aspects of the writer's role—especially as it is related to his status as an oppressed individual. Wright saw the problem in the following manner: The black writer had turned to writing in an attempt to demonstrate to the white world that there were "Negroes who were civilized." I suppose, here, he meant people like Charles Chestnutt and William Braithwaite. The writing, Wright attempted to prove, had become the voice of the educated Negro pleading with white America for justice. But it was "external to the lives of educated Negroes themselves." Further, much of this writing was rarely addressed to black people, to their needs, sufferings and aspirations.

It is precisely here that almost all of our literature had failed. It had succumbed merely to providing exotic entertainment for white America. As Wright suggests, we had yet to create a dynamic body of literature addressed to the needs of our people. And there are a myriad of socio-economic reasons underlying this failure. The so-called Harlem Renaissance was, for the most part, a fantasy-era for most black writers and their white friends. For the people of the community, it never even existed. It was a thing apart. And when the money stopped, in 1929, to quote Langston Hughes:

> We were no longer in vogue, anyway, we Negroes. Sophisticated New Yorkers turned to Noel Coward. Colored actors began to go hungry, publishers politely rejected new manuscripts, and patrons found other uses for their money. The cycle that had charlestoned into being on the dancing heels of "Shuf-

fle Along" now ended in "Green Pastures with De
Lawd." . . . The generous 1920's were over.

For most of us, they had never begun. It was all an illusion, a
kind of surrealistic euphoria.

Wright insisted on an approach to literature that would
reconcile the black man's "nationalism" and his "revolutionary
aspirations." The best way for the writer to do this, he wrote in
"Blue Print," was the utilization of his own tradition and
culture—a culture that had developed out of the black church,
and the folklore of the people:

> Blues, spirituals, and folk tales recounted from mouth
> to mouth; the whispered words of a black mother to
> her black daughter on the ways of men; the confiden-
> tial wisdom of a black father to his black son; the
> swapping of sex experiences on the street corners
> from boy to boy in the deepest vernacular; work
> songs sung under blazing suns—all these formed the
> channels through which the racial wisdom flowed.

And what of the nationalism about which we spoke earlier?
Here, again, the tension arises. The question of nationalism
occurs repeatedly in the works of Wright. Like DuBois and
other intellectuals, Wright found that he could not ignore it.
Within Wright himself, there was being waged a great conflict
over the validity of nationalism. In the essay under discussion,
he forces the question out into the open, asserting the necessity of understanding the function of nationalism in the lives of
the people:

> Let those who shy at the nationalistic implications
> of Negro life look at the body of folklore, living and
> powerful, which rose out of a common fate. Here are
> those vital beginnings of a recognition of a value in
> life as it is lived, a recognition that makes the emer-
> gence of a new culture in the shell of the old. And at
> the moment that this process starts, at the moment
> when people begin to realize a meaning in their
> suffering, the civilization that engenders that suffer-
> ing is doomed.

A further reading of this essay reveals that Wright was not trying to construct a black ideology, but was, instead, attempting a kind of reconciliation between nationalism and communism. The essay was written in 1937. By then, the Communists had discarded the "nation within a nation" concept and were working to discourage black nationalism among the Negro members of the party. Wright was trying to re-link nationalism and communism, but the two were incompatible. The Communists discouraged the construction of a black theoretical frame of reference, but did not substitute a theory that was more viable than the one some of its black party members proposed. Hence, the double-consciousness was not resolved. Wright ended up splitting with the party to preserve his own identity.

Even though he had failed, Richard Wright was headed in the right direction. But the conditions under which he labored did not allow success. The party, for example, had never really understood the "Negro question" in any manner that was finally meaningful to black people. Further, the nationalistic models which Wright and a contemporary of his Ralph Ellison saw around them were too "brutal" and "coarse" for their sensibilities (Ras, in Ellison's novel). Ultimately, the tension within Wright forced him to leave America, to become a voluntary exile.

The last years of his life were spent explaining the psychology of the oppressed throughout the Third World. In *White Man, Listen!*, he attempted to analyze, much like Fanon, the malaise accompanying the relationship between the oppressed and the oppressors. And the double consciousness never left him. *White Man, Listen!*, *Black Power*, and *The Color Curtain* are Wright's attempts to understand his own racial dilemma by placing it in an international context, thus linking it to the general effects of colonialism on the psychology of the oppressed. Therefore, these works historically link Wright with Garvey and DuBois, as well as foreshadow the ideas of Fanon and Brother Malcolm. More germane to our subject, these latter works are certainly more pertinent to the ideas of the "New Breed" youth than, say, *Native Son*.

They are especially more pertinent than Ralph Ellison's novel *Invisible Man*, which is a profound piece of writing but the kind of novel which, nonetheless, has little bearing on the world as the "New Breed" sees it. The things that concerned Ellison are interesting to read, but contemporary black youth feels another force in the world today. We know who we are, and we are not invisible, at least not to each other. We are not Kafkaesque creatures stumbling through a white light of confusion and absurdity. The light is black (now, get that!) as are most of the meaningful tendencies in the world.

> Let us waste no time in sterile litanies and nauseating mimicry. Leave this Europe where they are never done talking of Man, yet murder men everywhere they find them, at the corner of every one of their own streets, in all corners of the globe. For centuries they have stifled almost the whole of humanity in the name of a so-called spiritual experience. Look at them today swaying between atomic and spiritual disintegration. (Frantz Fanon, *The Wretched of the Earth*)

Our literature, our art, and our music are moving closer to the forces motivating black America. You can hear it everywhere, especially in the music, a surging new sound. Be it the Supremes, James Brown, the Temptations, John Coltrane, or Albert Ayler, there is a vital newness in this energy. There is love, tension and spiritual togetherness in it. We are beautiful— but there is more work to do, and just being beautiful is not enough.

We must take this sound, and make this energy meaningful to our people. Otherwise, it will have meant nothing, will have affected nothing. The force of what we have to say can only be realized in action. Black literature must become an integral part of the community's life-style. And I believe that it must also be integral to the myths and experiences underlying the total history of black people.

New constructs will have to be developed. We will have to alter our concepts of what art is, of what it is supposed to "do." The dead forms taught most writers in the white man's schools will have to be destroyed, or at best, radically altered. We can learn more about what poetry is by listening to the cadences in Malcolm's speeches than from most of Western poetics. Listen to James Brown scream. Ask yourself, then: Have you ever heard a Negro poet sing like that? Of course not, because we have been tied to the texts, like most white poets. The text could be destroyed and no one would be hurt in the least by it. The key is in the music. Our music has always been far ahead of our literature. Actually, until recently, it was our only literature, except for, perhaps, the folktale.

Therefore, what we are asking for is a new synthesis; a new sense of literature as a living reality. But first, we must liberate ourselves, destroy the double consciousness. We must integrate with ourselves, understand that we have within us a great vision, revolutionary and spiritual in nature, understanding that the West is dying and offers little promise of rebirth.

All of her prophets have told her so: Sartre, Brecht, Camus, Albee, Burroughs, and Fellini have foretold her doom. Can we do anything less? It is merely what we have always secretly known—what Garvey, DuBois, Fanon, and Malcolm knew: The West is dying, as it must, as it should. However, the approach of this death merely makes the power-mad Magogs of the West more vicious, more dangerous—like McNamara with his computing machines, scientifically figuring out how to kill more people. We must address ourselves to this reality in the sharpest terms possible. Primarily, it is an address to black people. And that is not protest, as such. You don't have to protest to a hungry man about his hunger. You have either to feed him, or help him to eliminate the root causes of that hunger.

What of craft—the writer's craft? Well, under the terms of a new definition concerning the function of literature, a new concept of what craft is will also evolve. For example, do I not find the craft of Stevie Wonder more suitable than that of Jascha Heifetz? Are not the sensibilities which produced the former closer to me than the latter? And does not the one indicate a way into things absent from the other?

To reiterate, the key to where the black people have to go is in the music. Our music has always been the most dominant manifestation of what we are and feel, literature was just an afterthought, the step taken by the Negro bourgeoisie who desired acceptance on the white man's terms. And that is precisely why the literature has failed. It was the case of one elite addressing another elite.

But our music is something else. The best of it has always operated at the core of our lives, forcing itself upon us as in a ritual. It has always, somehow, represented the collective psyche. Black literature must attempt to achieve that same sense of the collective ritual, but ritual directed at the destruction of useless, dead ideas. Further, it can be a ritual that affirms our highest possibilities, but is yet honest with us.

Some of these tendencies already exist in the literature. It is readily perceivable in LeRoi Jones's *Black Mass,* and in a recent recording of his with the Jihad Singers. Also, we have the work of Yusuf Rahman, who is the poetic equivalent of Charlie Parker. Similar tendencies are found in Sun Ra's music and poetry; Ronald Fair's novel *Many Thousand Gone;* the short stories of Henry Dumas; the poetry of K. Kgositsile, Welton Smith, Ed Spriggs, and Rolland Snellings [Askia Toure]; the dramatic choreography of Eleo Pomare; Calvin Hernton's very explosive poems; Ishmael Reed's poetry and prose works, which are notable for a startling display of imagery; David Henderson's work, particularly "Keep on Pushin'," where he gets a chance to sing. There are many, many others.

What this has all been leading us to say is that the poet must become a performer, the way James Brown is a performer— loud, gaudy, and racy. He must take his work where his people are: Harlem, Watts, Philadelphia, Chicago, and the rural South. He must learn to embellish the context in which the work is executed; and where possible, link the work to all usable aspects of the music. For the context of the work is as important as the work itself. Poets must learn to sing, dance and chant their works, tearing into the substance of their individual and collective experiences. We must make literature move people to a deeper understanding of what this thing is all about, be a kind of priest, a black magician, working juju with the word on the world.

Finally, the black artist must link his work to the struggle for his liberation and the liberation of his brothers and sisters. But, he will have executed an essential aspect of his role if he makes even a small gesture in the manner outlined. He will be furthering the psychological liberation of his people, without which no change is even possible.

The artist and the political activist are one. They are both shapers of the future reality. Both understand and manipulate the collective myths of the race. Both are warriors, priests, lovers, and destroyers. For the first violence will be internal— the destruction of a weak spiritual self for a more perfect self. But it will be a necessary violence. It is the only thing that will destroy the double consciousness—the tension that is in the souls of the black folk.

1968*

NOTE

1. Herzl (1860–1904) and Weizmann (1874–1952) are two important thinkers in the history of Jewish Zionism. During the nineteenth century, Jewish intellectuals began to describe analytically the problem of the Jews since what is called the Diaspora—the dispersion of the Jews among the Gentiles after the Exile. The efforts of these two men and many others culminated in the erection of Israel. Because Garvey also advocated a "return," some writers have called his movement "Black Zionism."

*The date at the end of an essay refers to the year of first publication.

The Black Writer's Role, I
Richard Wright

What is the role of the black writer in these intense political times? This question has been asked before, and it will continue being asked until the writer comes up with a satisfactory and workable answer—something he has failed to do. It is pathetic that considering the present crisis with which black people are faced, this question has not been settled in a manner that suits the collective needs of black people. The writer must accept the responsibility of guiding the spiritual and cultural life of his people. He must begin to evolve his techniques and forms in light of the black community's needs. So far, we have only had confusion. Intelligent men like Ralph Ellison, whose *Invisible Man* is an important novel, have further complicated the issues by either isolating themselves from the community, or by advocating Western critical theories which, finally, concede to a non-functional, actionless concept of literary art. This society must be changed. The writer must be a part of that change. He must be the conscience and spirit of that change. The black writer must understand that his destiny as an artist is ultimately bound up with, and integral to, all other aspects of the human condition.

Protest Literature

Richard Wright's novel *Native Son* is usually referred to as an example of "protest literature." I, personally, find this designation slightly inaccurate, but for the purposes of this article will not enter into a polemic that would further cloud the issue. James Baldwin wrote an essay entitled *Everybody's Protest*

Novel, in which he attempted to analyze and explain the basic shallowness of the protest novel, the worst example of which is Harriet Beecher Stowe's *Uncle Tom's Cabin.* However, Baldwin made the mistake of placing or implying that *Native Son* is somewhere in the same category. In his book *Nobody Knows My Name,* Baldwin explains how this essay affected his friendship with Richard Wright:

> I had mentioned Richard's *Native Son* at the end of the essay because it was the most important and most celebrated novel of Negro life to have appeared in America. Richard thought that I had attacked it, whereas, as far as I was concerned, I had scarcely criticized it.

Wright considered the essay not only as an attack upon him but an attack on all American Negroes because he felt the "idea of protest literature" was being attacked. It is my opinion, and I will return to this later, that Wright and Baldwin both missed the point. The black writer's problem really grows out of a confusion about function, rather than a confusion about form. Once he has understood the concrete relationship between himself and society, then the question of form can be seen differently. He will then be forced to question the validity of the forms that have been forced upon him by society, and construct new ones.

Native Son is a classic of modern American literature. Its impact on Afro-American writing is still being felt. Upon publication in 1940, it was the subject of almost violent debates; especially between black and white members of the Communist party to which Wright belonged. These debates and exchanges touched on every aspect of the novel, from its use of violence to what some saw as a "lack of proletarian consciousness." Wright's popular novel exposed America to its malignancy; a malignancy festering beneath the blackface image of the dancing Negro smiling and making love in his *Nigger Heaven.* Its message was a harsh one. And everyone who read *Native Son* was, in some way, affected by it. Bigger Thomas— Wright's damned hero—became the most famous Negro in American fiction, except, perhaps, for Nigger Jim in *Huckle-*

berry Finn. However, Bigger was no clown, no loving father figure to play pranks on; but a confused and frightened product of the slums of North America. Driven and urged on to violence out of a fear stemming from the black man's first contact with the West, Bigger is forced to commit two murders: First he murders the liberal daughter of a white philanthropist, then his own girl whose knowledge of Bigger's crime also makes her dangerous. Who, the novel asks, is responsible for these murders? Bigger? Did he create the situation which lead to the murders? Who made him and his people live like rats, and finally die like rats? *Native Son* asked these questions in an impassioned manner that could not be ignored. It opened up a strong movement among writers like Chester Himes and Willard Motley. Ellison himself refers to Wright as a "literary cousin." *Native Son* is considered throughout the world as one of America's greatest literary achievements.

Wright's Attitude about the Role of the Writer

Native Son was a great success. But what did Wright feel was the role of the black writer? Was there a special role consigned to the black writer? Or were his problems purely asethetic— concerned essentially with the traditional problems of craft and literary excellence? Does politics have anything to do with the black writer's role? What about an Afro-American culture—an Afro-American tradition, do these have any bearing on the problems confronting black writers? Wright dealt with these questions very early in his career. We believe—that to some extent—he provided valuable answers to these questions, even if he himself was never able to put them into practice.

In 1937, *New Challenge*, a little magazine that had sprung out of the "Negro Renaissance" published an essay by Wright entitled "Blue Print for Negro Writing." It is one of the most important essays on the role of the Negro writer. In it Wright clearly defines all aspects of the black writer's role, especially as it is related to his status as an oppressed individual.

Wright saw the problem in this manner: The Negro writer had taken to writing as an attempt to demonstrate to the white world that there were some Negroes who were "civilized." Or it (the writing) had become the voice of the educated Negro pleading with white America for justice. The writing, "was external to the lives of educated Negroes themselves." The best of this writing was rarely addressed to the Negro, his needs, his sufferings, his aspirations.

Here is the criterion on which this series is based. It is precisely here that almost all Afro-American literature has failed. Our literature has succumbed to the role of merely providing entertainment to white people. We have failed to create a dynamic body of Afro-American literature addressed, as Wright suggests, to the suffering, needs, and aspirations of black people. The black writer is, generally, caught up in the artistic standard of Western capitalistic society. He is a divided person, confused between loyalty to his own people or to the oppressing society. His is a desire to be accepted on his own terms. Rather than on those forced upon him by white critics and others who are not aware of his problems. Every black writer is, somehow, engaged in a battle with himself to discover, his own dynamic *vis-à-vis* his status as an artist and a member of an oppressed group. Wright's essay suggests that the writer circumvent this problem by accepting his responsibility to his people.

He was insisting upon an approach to Afro-American literature which reconciled the black man's "nationalism" and his "revolutionary aspirations." The best way for the writer to do this was to utilize his own tradition and culture. A culture which had developed out of the Negro church, and the folklore of the Negro people. About the church, Wright explains:

> It was through the portals of the church that the American Negro first entered the shrine of western culture. Living under slave conditions of life, bereft of his African heritage, the Negroes' struggle for religion on the plantations between 1820–1860 assumed the form of a struggle for human rights. It remained a relatively revolutionary struggle until religion began to serve as an antidote for suffering and denial.

But it was in his folklore that the black man achieved his most "indigenous and complete expression":

> Blues, spirituals, and folk tales recounted from mouth to mouth; the whispered words of a black mother to

her black daughter on the ways of men; the confidential wisdom of a black father to his black son; the swapping of sex experiences on street corners from boy to boy in the deepest vernacular; work songs sung under blazing suns—all these formed the channels through which the racial wisdom flowed.

If the writer was to address his people, it would be necessary for him to understand their culture, in order that the people would implicitly feel their place in his work, or message.

Nationalism

What about "nationalism"? Here Wright ran into some significant difficulties. The question of nationalism occurs repeatedly in the works of Richard Wright. It is clear that within Wright himself there was a great conflict being waged over the validity of nationalism. In the essay now under discussion, "Blue Print for Negro Writing," he forces the question into the open by asserting the necessity of black people recognizing the collective nature of their struggle:

> Let those who shy at the nationalist implications of Negro life look at the body of folklore, living and powerful, which rose out of a common fate. Here are those vital beginnings of a recognition of a value in life as it is lived, a recognition that makes the emergence of a new culture in the shell of the old. And at the moment that this process starts, at the moment when a people begin to realize a *meaning* in their suffering, the civilization that engenders that suffering is doomed.

This statement is clearly in support of nationalism. But a further reading of the essay reveals that Wright really had not decided that the issue of nationalism exists paramount to other political ones. Namely, Wright's involvement in the Communist party. The party had a policy of discouraging nationalism. In "The God That Failed," Wright tells how a friend of his was expelled from the party on the grounds that he was too nationalistic:

"Dick," he said, "Ross is a nationalist." He paused
to let the weight of his accusation sink in. He meant
that Ross's militancy was extreme. "We Communists
don't dramatize Negro nationalism," he said in a
voice that laughed, accused and drawled.

Therefore, "Blue Print for Negro Writing" attempts a kind of
reconciliation between nationalism and communism. In some
respects Wright succeeds. For the nationalism that Wright is
concerned with is a nationalism of action. American communism, with its ideology of action, was a significant force in the
development of black writers and intellectuals. But it proved to
be harmful to the long-range developments of an organized and
cohesive outlook among black people. For the party drained off
the best of the Negro intelligentsia, and channelled their energies into areas that have proved particularly uncreative—uncreative in terms of unifying black people into a force that
could decide their own destiny.

But Wright understand the necessities and realities of nationalism when he says:

There is, however, a culture of the Negro which is
his and has been addressed to him; a culture which
has, for good or ill, helped to clarify his consciousness and create emotional attitudes which are condu-
cive to action.

This action must arise for black people out of a common sense
of destiny and purpose. The artist must utilize that culture to
enable black people to realize that destiny and purpose in a
collective fashion. Richard Wright attempted to lay a theoretical foundation on which future Afro-American writing could
be based. This writer feels that most of what Wright had to
say about these matters is valid, but that it needs further
examination.

1965

The Black Writer's Role, II
Ellison's Zoot Suit

Well, there is one thing that you have to admit. And that is dealing with Ralph Ellison is no easy matter. It is no easy task to fully characterize the nature of Ellison's life and work. He cannot be put into any one bag and conveniently dispensed with. Any attempt to do so merely leads to aesthetic and ideological oversimplifications. On the surface, oversimplifications may appear pragmatic and viable but, in the long run, they weaken us. To overlook the complex dimensions of a man's ideas, character, and personality is to do great disservice to the righteous dissemination of knowledge.

Much of the criticism directed against Ellison is personal, oversimplified, and often not based on an analysis of the man's work and ideas. A great deal of the criticism emanates from ideological sources that most of us today reject.

To be concise, much of the anti-Ellison criticism springs from a specific body of Marxian and black neo-Marxian thought. The literary term used to designate this body of thought is called "social realism." Some of Ellison's most virulent critics have been social realists.

One of the most famous of social realist attacks was the subject of a literary exchange between Ellison and Irving Howe, a liberal left-winger and former editor of *Dissent* magazine. In an essay published in the Fall 1963 issue of *Dissent*, Howe accused Baldwin and Ralph Ellison of abandoning the task of the Negro writer. That task Howe proposed to be the militant assertion of Negro freedom. In his assault upon Baldwin and Ellison, Howe evoked Richard Wright as the embodiment of the truest, most relevant exponent of black freedom in fiction. Howe, the knowing white boy, praised Wright for his penchant toward what is termed "protest" literature and castigated both Ellison and Baldwin for their failure to carry on the "protest" tradition as exemplified by Wright's *Native Son*.

Ellison wrote an excellent rebuttal to Howe's piece titled "The World and the Jug."[1] Ellison attacked Howe's attempt to rigidly circumscribe the role of the black writer. He asserted the essential differences in outlook between himself and Richard Wright. Where Wright, in *Black Boy*, saw black life "void of hope" and bare of tradition, Ellison countered with a very positive vision of Afro-American life. For Ellison, black people did not exhibit a tradition void of hopes, memories, and personal attachments. They were, instead, profoundly human and blessed with a strong, spiritually sustaining culture. "The World and the Jug" is a finely balanced essay, mean, but eloquently controlled.

Underlying this exchange between Ellison and Howe is the recurring question of the writer's role, especially in the context of the struggle for human liberation. Marxism puts forth the idea that all literature is propaganda, or becomes propaganda when it enters the social sphere. And, as propaganda, it is implicitly a reflection of class attitudes. The role of the revolutionary writer in the Marxist context is, therefore, to extol the virtues of the proletariat, to sharpen their class consciousness in order that they may overthrow the ruling classes and finally take control of the "means of production."

Richard Wright was especially influenced by the Marxist ideas he encountered in the thirties. As a young writer he had joined the John Reed Club in Chicago and was very active in Communist cultural activities. Coming from Mississippi, where he had seen and experienced racial oppression, he sincerely believed that it was his duty to use his writing as a weapon against that oppression. All of his writing, up to and including his masterwork *Native Son*, is informed by his belief in social revolution. Following Lenin's idea that the revolutionary vanguard must expose the corruption in the capitalist system, all of Wright's fictional landscapes, with the exception of *The Long Dream*, tend to be very bleak and humorless. Excellent social realist that he was, he was skillful at depicting in exact detail the impact of the material world on both the oppressed and the oppressors alike. Now Wright has gone the way of the ancestors, but he is still a major influence in contemporary black writing. At least we are still feeling the influence of a certain kind of "protest" writing that appears highly reminiscent of Wright, even though most of it does not begin to approach Wright's high level of artistic achievement.

What Ralph Ellison was doing in his exchange with Irving Howe was defending his right to his (Ellison's) own personal vision, while trying not to fall into the bag of depreciating Wright: "Must I be condemned because my sense of Negro Life was quite different?" (S&A, 119). Ellison asks this question, fully aware that there is an ideological contingent lying in wait to pounce on him for not carrying on in the tradition of Wright. But, ironically, it was Wright himself who rejected the sectarian Marxism of the American Communist party. Dig his essay alongside Arthur Koestler's in *The God That Failed*. And in the foreword to George Padmore's *Pan-Africanism or Communism*, Wright implies that the black man operates on the premise of a personal nationalism, and not along fixed ideological lines:

> The Negro's fundamental loyalty is, therefore, to *himself*. His situation makes this inevitable. [Am I letting awful secrets out of the bag? I'm sorry. The time has come for this problem to be stated clearly so that there is no possibility of further misunderstanding or confusion. The Negro, even when embracing Communism or Western Democracy, is not supporting ideologies; he is seeking to use *instruments* (instruments owned and controlled by men of other races!) for his own ends. He stands outside of those instruments and ideologies; he has to do so, for he is not allowed to blend with them in a natural, organic and healthy manner.] (13)

Like Wright, Ellison was also active in the literary Left of the late thirties and early forties. And also like Wright, Ellison rejected sectarian Marxism. As far as I can perceive, Ellison had never really internalized Marxism in the first place. This appears to be the case even when he was writing in the left-wing *New Masses*. His work appears always to have been striving for a penetration into those areas of black life-style that exist below the mere depiction of external oppression. He had read Marx, though, as should anyone who is interested in those ideas operative in today's world. But luckily for us, his work never took on the simplistic assertions of the literary Marxist.

Therefore, Ellison's clearly articulated break with naturalism must also be seen in light of his previous awareness that hard-core ideologues, particularly Communists, represented an awesome threat not only to his artistic sensibility, but to his "national" sensibility as well. And it is amazing how fantastically true Ellison's initial impulses have been. If Harold Cruse's *Crisis of the Negro Intellectual* has any one theme that demands our greatest attention, it is his clear analysis of the detrimental role that the left wing has played in our struggle for self-determination and liberation. Ellison himself is also aware, and this awareness underlies the following remarks he made in an interview that was published in the March 1967 issue of *Harper's* magazine. He is speaking to several young black writers:

> They fostered the myth that Communism was twentieth-century Americanism, but to be a twentieth-century American meant, in their thinking, that you had to be more Russian than American and less Negro than either. That's how they lost the Negroes. The Communists recognized no plurality of interests and were really responding to the necessities of Soviet foreign policy and when the war came, Negroes got caught and were made expedient in the shifting of policy. Just as Negroes who fool around with them today are going to get caught in the next turn of the screw. ("Stern Discipline," 88)

Ellison has not been forgotten by his enemies both in the white Left and the black Left. The Communists were the first to lead the attack against Ellison when *Invisible Man* appeared in 1952. Since then, we have read or heard a number of attacks emanating from black writers who trace their literary lineage from the so-called progressive movements of the thirties and forties. In this connection, the interested reader should dig

Harold Cruse's section on Ellison in *The Crisis of the Negro Intellectual*. Cruse's book seems theoretically out of focus in many instances because it walks such a precarious line between a weakly defined nationalism and a strained neo-Marxism. But, in my opinion, he is strictly on the case when he enters the "debate" between Ellison and his detractors. Here I refer to Cruse's account of the anti-Ellison attack that occurred at a writers' conference at the New School in 1965. Leading the charge against Ellison were Herbert Aptheker, a leading theoretician of the Communist party; John Henrik Clarke, the editor of several significant anthologies; and John O. Killens, the novelist. Cruse asserts that the writers gathered at the conference were not properly prepared to cope with the questions posed by Ellison's critical and aesthetic methodology. Further, he asserted that "the radical left wing will never forgive Ellison for writing *Invisible Man*" (Cruse, 505–511).

Why? The answer is quite simple. The literary Left, both white and Negro, were fuming over Ellison's rejection of white-controlled left-wing politics, his harsh depiction of the Communists (called the "Brotherhood" in Ellison's novel), and the novel's obvious rejection of the aesthetics of social realism. The Communist *Daily Worker* of June 1, 1952, for example, published a review of the book under the following headline:

RALPH ELLISON'S NOVEL "INVISIBLE MAN" SHOWS SNOBBERY, CONTEMPT FOR NEGRO PEOPLE

The review which followed was written by a Negro left-winger named Abner N. Berry, who opened his piece by stating:

> Written in vein of middle class snobbishness—even contempt—towards the Negro people, Ellison's work manipulates his nameless hero for 439 pages through a maze of corruption, brutality, anticommunism slanders, sex perversion and the sundry inhumanities upon which a dying social system feeds.

And on the aesthetic level he asserted:

> There are no *real* characters in *Invisible Man*, nor are there any *realistic* situations. The structure, the

characters and the situations are *contrived* and re-
semble *fever fantasy*. . . . In effect, it is 439 pages of
contempt for humanity, written in an *affected,
pretentious,* and *other worldly* style to suit the king
pins of world white supremacy. (Emphasis mine,
naturally.)

Therefore, along with making the unpardonable sin of ob-
liquely attacking the party through his characterization of the
"Brotherhood" in his novel, Ellison was also being attacked for
having developed a new aesthetic universe, one that was seeking to develop its own laws of form and content. Social realism,
particularly Marxist socialist realism, does not allow for the free
play of fantasy and myth that Ellison was attempting in his
novel. Marxist social realism essentially posits the view that the
details of a work of art should be predicated on fairly simple
structural lines. A work should extol the virtues of the working
classes; but, the extolling should take place along party lines.
Hence, not only is the writer's aesthetic range controlled, but
his political range as well. And to further worsen matters, this
aesthetic ideology is nearly Victorian in the extreme. It seems
to emanate from a very square vision of social realities.

Here is John O. Killens in the June 1952 edition of the
newspaper *Freedom* commenting on *Invisible Man:*

Mix a heavy portion of sex and a heavy, heavy portion of violence, a bit of sadism and a dose of redbaiting
(Blame the Communists for everything bad) and you
have the making of a bestseller today.

Add to this decadent mixture . . . a Negro theme
with Negro characters as Uncle Toms, pimps, sex
perverts, guilt-ridden traitors—and you have a pub-
lisher's dream.

But how does Ellison present the Negro people?
The thousands of exploited farmers in the South represented by a sharecropper who made both his wife
and daughter pregnant. The main character of the
book is a young Uncle Tom who is obsessed with
getting to the "top" by pleasing the Big, Rich White
folks. A million Negro veterans who fought against
facism in World War II are rewarded with a madden-

ing chapter [of] crazy vets running hogwild in a down home tavern. The Negro ministry is depicted by an Ellison character who is a Harlem pastor and at the same time a pimp and a numbers racketeer.

The Negro people need Ralph Ellison's *Invisible Man* like we need a hole in the head or a stab in the back.

It is a vicious distortion of Negro life.[2]

It is remarkable how similar Berry's and Killens's reactions were to this novel. They easily could have been written by the same person. But this is supposed to be 1970. And I would like to believe that we can read *Invisible Man* with more intellectual freedom than is apparent in Abner Berry's and John O. Killens's presumably sincere, but extremely flaccid critical remarks. Especially today, when the major concerns ramified throughout Ellison's life and work are still very relevant to our contemporary search for new systems of social organization and creative values. Ellison's vision, in some respects, is not that far removed from the ideas of some of the best black writers and intellectuals working today. That's why I wince somewhat when I reread the following statement that I made in the afterword to *Black Fire:* "The things that concerned Ellison are interesting to read, but contemporary Black youth feel another force in the world today. We know who we are, and are not invisible, *at least not to each other*. We are not Kafkaesque creatures stumbling through a white light of confusion and absurdity. . . ." (652).

My statements represent one stage in a long series of attempts, over the past several years, to deal with the fantastic impression that Ellison's work has had on my life. It is now my contention that of all the so-called older black writers working today, it is Ralph Ellison who is the most engaging. But the major issue separating many young black writers from a Ralph Ellison appears to have very little to do with creative orientation, but much more to do with the question of political activism and the black writer. Ellison's stance is decidedly nonpolitical: "[The novel] is *always* a public gesture, though not necessarily a political one" (S&A, 110). (We'll come back to this later.) And further, there is a clearly "aristocratic" impulse in his stance, an understandable desire not to be soiled by the riffraff from all kinds of ideological camps. As we have already noted, Ellison, like Wright, was active in left-wing literary circles in the late thirties and early forties. There must have been some psyhological torments for him then, since we can glean, even from his early writings, a distinctly "nationalistic" orientation that must have, at times, been at odds with the party line. Why should this have caused problems?

The answer is very simple. Most serious writers should understand it: The left wing, particularly the Communist party, represented one of the main means by which a young black writer could get published. There were perhaps other routes through the Establishment. But for a young black writer checking out the literary happenings in 1937 (Ellison was about twenty-eight years old when he wrote his first piece for *New Challenge*, a black, Left-oriented magazine), the party was very attractive. After all, was not Richard Wright on that side of the street? And did not the Communist party seem very amenable to young black talent? I hope that I am not exaggerating, but it seems that, from this perspective, the whole literary atmosphere, for a black writer, seems to have been dominated by the Left.

Never having been a hard-core ideologue in the first place, Ellison appears to have been exceedingly uncomfortable as a leftist polemicist. Some of his journalistic writing for the Communist-oriented *New Masses* strains for political and social relevancy, just as some of ours does. But you can perceive another kind of spirit trying to cut through the Marxist phrasemongering, another kind of spirit trying to develop a less simplistic, more viable attitude toward not only the usable content of Afro-American culture in America, but more important, a sense of the *meaning* of that culture's presence and its manifestations as they impinged upon "white culture." One isolatable political tendency that begins to emerge at the end of Ellison's Marxist period is a nascent, loosely structured form of black nationalism.

But Ellison was always clever. As Ellison himself notes in the *Harper's* interview quoted earlier, he never wrote the "official type of fiction." "I wrote," he says, "what might be alled propaganda—having to do with the Negro struggle—but my fiction was always trying to be something else: something different even from Wright's fiction. I never accepted the ideology which the *New Masses* attempted to impose on writers. They hated Dostoevski, but I was studying Dostoevski. . . . I was studying [Henry] James. I was also reading Marx, Gorki, Sholokhov, and Isaac Babel. I was reading everything, including the Bible. Most of all, I was reading Malraux. . . . This is where I was really living at the time. . . . Anyway, I think style is more important than political ideologies" ("Stern Discipline," 86).

But there is even a counter-Marxian thrust below the surface of his early political writings. This counterthrust manifests itself in Ellison's concern with folk culture and life-style. So that in the midst of his political writings, it is possible to see him groping for a unique cultural theory, one that is shaped on the basis of cultural imperatives integral to the black man's experience in America. For example, 1943 found Ellison managing editor of the *Negro Quarterly*. The editor was Angelo Herndon, a black intellectual of the radical Left. Herndon had been arrested in the South for engaging in union activities. The *Negro Quarterly* appears to have been the last attempt on the part of black intellectuals of that period to fashion an ideological position that was revolutionary but not totally dominated by the white Marxist Left.

But there was a war going on in 1943. When the war began, America found herself on the side of the Allied forces, Britain and France. She was also allied with the Russians against the facist German state. Now that socialist Russia was under attack, American Communists began to concentrate on the war effort. In the interim between the Russo-German Pact of 1939 and the formal entry of Russia into the war, there had been a significant shift in party policy with respect to the "Negro question." Now that Russia was under attack, the Nonaggression Pact abrogated, the Communist party was urging its American chapter to de-emphasize the struggle for Negro liberation and instead to concentrate on the war effort. They correctly reasoned that excessive political activism among black people would only slow down the industrial war machinery, thus endangering Russia by impeding the progress of the Allied struggle in Europe. All of this put left-wing black intellectuals in a trick.

Their international perspective forced them to acknowledge the awesome threat that fascism posed to human progress. But they were also acutely aware that an atmosphere of racism and fascism also existed here in America. Then there was the question of Japan. Many black people felt a vague sense of identification with the powerful Asian nation and secretly wished that she would overcome the white Western powers. And there were other attitudes which grew out of the specific situation of racism in America.

A significant item in this regard is an unsigned editorial that appeared in the *Negro Quarterly* in 1943 which, from the import of its style and content, is believed to have been written by Ralph Ellison. The editorial addresses itself to the conflicting attitudes held by black people toward the war effort. Black people were being segregated in the armed services, and, because of racism, were not even getting an opportunity to make some bread in the war-related industries. It was the latter situation which had led to A. Philip Randolph's 1941 threat to march on Washington for jobs and fair employment. Under Randolph's pressure, President Franklin D. Roosevelt was forced to sign Executive Order 8802, which was supposed to guarantee black people equal access to jobs in the war industries. Under these circumstances, it is easy to understand why there were, among black people, such conflicting attitudes toward the war.

Ellison's writings enumerated these attitudes. They ranged from apathy to all-out rejection of war. Addressing himself to this attitude of rejection in the editorial mentioned earlier, Ellison stated that it sprang from a "type of Negro nationalism which, in a sense, is admirable; it would settle all problems on the simple principle that Negroes deserve equal treatment with all other free human beings." But Ellison concluded that this attitude of total rejection of the war effort was too narrow in scope. It was not just a case of "good white men" against "bad white men." The Negro, he strongly asserted, had a natural stake in the defeat of fascism, whether it was national or international. He further proposed that there was another manifestation of "Negro nationalism" that was neither a "blind acceptance" of the war nor an "unqualified rejection" of it. This attitude is

broader and more human than the first two attitudes; and it is *scientific* enough to make use of *both*
by *transforming* them into *strategies of struggle*. It is
committed to life, it holds that the main task of the
Negro people is to work unceasingly toward creating
those democratic conditions in which it can live and
recreate itself. It believes the historical role of Negroes to be that of integrating the larger American
nation and compelling it untiringly toward true freedom. And while it will have none of the slavishness
of the first attitude, it is imaginative and flexible
enough to die if dying is forced upon it. (Emphasis
mine.)

Somehow we are involved here with an attempt at ideological
reconciliation between two contending trends in Afro-American
thought, that is, the will toward self-definition, exclusive of the
overall white society, and at the same time the desire not to be
counted out of the processes of so-called American democracy.
This is the precarious balancing act that Ellison is forced to
perform while he tries to cut through the ideological prison in
which he finds himself encased. He attacks Negro leaders for
not having group consciousness, and calls for a "centralization"
of Negro political power.

But as we proceed to read the editorial, we begin to encounter the Ellison who would be himself and write one of the most
important novels in history. Toward the end of this editorial,
with its carefully balanced blend of Marxism and Negro nationalism, we find Ellison making the following blatantly non-
Marxist statement:

A third major problem, and one that is indispens-
able to the centralization and direction of power, is
that of learning the meaning of the *myths* and *symbols*
which abound among the Negro masses. For without
this knowledge, leadership, no matter how correct its
program, will fail. Much in Negro life remains a
mystery; perhaps the *zoot suit conceals* profound
political meaning; perhaps the symmetrical frenzy of
the Lindy-hop conceals clues to great potential
powers—if only Negro leaders would solve this *riddle*.
On this knowledge depends the effectiveness of any

slogan or tactic. For instance, it is obvious that Negro resentment over their treatment at the hands of
their allies is justified. This naturally makes for a
resistance to our stated war aims, even though these
aims are essentially correct; and they will be accepted by the Negro masses only to the extent that
they are helped to see the bright star of *their own*
hopes through the *fog* of their daily experiences. The
problem is *psychological*; it will be solved only by a
Negro leadership that is aware of the psychological
attitudes and incipient forms of action which the
black masses *reveal* in their emotion-charged *myths*,
symbols, and wartime *folk-lore*. Only through a skillful and wise manipulation of these centers of re-
pressed social energy will Negro resentments, self-pity
and indignation be channelized to cut through temporary issues and become transformed into positive
action. This is not to make the problem simply one of
words, but to recognize . . . that words have their
own vital importance. (Emphasis mine.)

There is a clear, definite sense of cultural nationalism at work
here. These statements represent an especial attempt on the
part of Ellison to get past the simplistic analysis of folk culture
brought to bear on the subject by Marxist social realists. For
rather than locating the mechanisms for organizing political
power totally in an analysis of the black man's class structure,
Ellison turns Marxism on its head, and makes the manipulation
of cultural mechanisms the basis for black liberation.[3] Further,
these statements set into motion a host of themes which are
elaborated upon in his later work, particularly his cultural
criticism. Here also we get snatches of a theory of culture. And
some aspect of this theory seems to imply that there is an
unstated, even noumenal set of values that exists beneath the
surface of black American culture.

These values manifest themselves in a characteristic manner,
or an *expressive style*. The Lindy Hop and the zoot suit are,
therefore, in this context not merely social artifacts, but they,
in fact, mask deeper levels of symbolic and social energy.
Ellison perceives this theory as the instrumental basis for a
new kind of Negro leader:

They [the leaders] must integrate themselves with
the Negro masses; they must be constantly alert to
new concepts, new techniques and new trends among
peoples and nations with an eye toward appropriat-
ing those which are valid when tested against the
reality of Negro life. By the same test they must be
just as alert to reject the faulty programs of their
friends. When needed concepts, techniques or theories do not exist they must create them. Many new
concepts will evolve when the people are closely
studied in action.

To some extent, this kind of perception shapes many of the
characters in *Invisible Man*. Rinehart comes to mind in this
connection. However, there is a specific allusion to the ideas
enunciated in this 1943 editorial in the following passage from
Ellison's novel:

What about those fellows waiting still and silent
there on the platform, so still and silent they clash
with the crowd in their very immobility, standing
noisy in their very silence; harsh as a cry of terror in
their quietness? What about these three boys, coming now along the platform, tall and slender, walking
stiffly with swinging shoulders in their well-pressed,
too-hot-for-summer suits, their collars high and tight
about their necks, their identical hats of black cheap
felt set upon the crowns of their heads with a severe
formality above their conked hair? It was as though
I'd never seen their like before: Walking slowly,
their shoulders swaying, their legs swinging from
their hips in trousers that ballooned upward from
cuffs fitting snug about their ankles; their coats long
and hip-tight with shoulders far too broad to be those
of natural western men. These fellows whose bodies
seemed—what had one of my teachers said of me?
—"You're like one of these African sculptures, dis-
torted in the interest of design." Well, what design
and whose? [4]

To the protagonist, they seem like "dancers in a funeral service." (This episode follows the death of Tod Clifton.) Their

black faces are described as being "secret." They wear "heel-plated shoes" and rhythmically tap as they walk. They are said to be "men outside of historical time." That is to say, no current theory of historical development accurately describes them. Yet there is a gnawing and persistent feeling on the part of the unnamed protagonist that the boys may hold the key to the future liberation. And as he grasps the implications of this idea, he is emotionally shaken:

> But who knew (and now I began to tremble so violently I had to lean against a refuse can)—who knew but they were the *saviors*, the *true leaders, the bearers* of something precious? The *stewards* of something uncomfortable, burdensome, which they hated because, living outside of history, *there was no one to applaud their value* and they themselves failed to understand it. (*IM*, 333; emphasis mine.)

Ellison's 1943 remark in the *Negro Quarterly* concerning black cultural compulsions were cloaked in the language of politics. But they implicitly penetrate way beyond the sphere of politics. It is obvious from the foregoing passage that he thought enough of the concept of hidden cultural compulsions in black American life to *translate* them into art. Further, as we have noted, the concept is rather non-Marxist in texture and in substance. It probably represents, for him, a "leap" not only in political consciousness but in aesthetic consciousness as well. As a result of his experiences with hard-core ideological constructs, Ellison came to feel that politics were essentially inhibiting to an artist, if they could not be subsumed into art. Perhaps, this is what he means when he says in the *Harper's* interview: "Anyway, I think style is more important than political ideologies" ("Stern Discipline," 86).

I am not sure whether I fully concur with Ellison on this point. But there is something in his stance that specifically relates to the current Black Arts Movement. The current movement is faced with some of the same problems that confronted Ellison. Only the historical landscape has changed, and the operational rhetoric is different.

I don't think I am exaggerating when I say that some form of nationalism is operative throughout all sections of the black community. The dominant political orientations shaping the sensibilities of many contemporary black writers fall roughly into the categories of cultural nationalism and revolutionary nationalism. That is to say, as writers, we owe whatever importance we may have to this current manifestation of nationalism. I, for one, tend to believe this is a good situation in which to be. It provides an audience to which to address our work, and also imparts to it a certain sense of contemporaneity and social relevance.

But we are going to have to be careful not to let our rhetoric obscure the fact that a genuine nationalist revolution in the arts will fail if the artistic products of that revolution do not encounter our audiences in a manner that demands their most profound attention. I'm talking about a black art that sticks to the ribs, an art that through the strength of all of its ingredients— form, content, craft, and technique—illuminates something specific about the living culture of the nation, and, by extension, reveals something fundamental about man on this planet.

Therefore, we have to resist the tendency to "program" our art, to set unnatural limitations upon it. To do so implies that we ultimately don't trust the intelligence of the national laity, and consequently feel that we must paternally guide them down the course of righteous blackness. So very often we defuse the art by shaping it primarily on the basis of fashionable political attitudes. There is a tendency to respond to work simply from the sensation it creates.[5] If black art is to survive, in the national sense, it's gonna need more supporting it than a cluster of new clichés.

Translating Politics into Art

There is quite a discussion about the nature of history in Ellison's *Invisible Man*. Along with the obvious theme of identity, the nameless narrator is constantly in search of a "usable past." In order to arrive at an understanding of the complex dimensions of his American experience, Ellison plunged deep into the murky world of mythology and folklore, both of which are essential elements in the making of a people's history. But Ellison's history is nondialectical. The novel attempts to con-

ESSAYS 45

struct its own universe, based on its own imperatives, the
central ones being the shaping of a personal vision, as in the
blues, and the celebration of a collective vision as is represented by the living culture. And it is the living culture, with
all of its shifting complexities, which constitutes the essential
landscape of the novel. The unnamed narrator questions the
"scientific" history of the Brotherhood and, in one of the intense sections of the novel, asks the following question: "What
if Brother Jack were wrong? What if history was a gambler,
instead of a force in a laboratory experiment, and the boys his
ace in the hole? What if history was not a reasonable citizen,
but a madman full of paranoid guile . . . ?" (*IM*, 333)

This discourse follows the death of Tod Clifton, a man who
had previously been described as having fallen "outside of
history." Tottering between contending political forces, that
is, the rigid dogmas of the Brotherhood and the emotionally
compelling rhetoric of Ras the Exhorter, Tod attempts to leap
outside historical time altogether. And he ultimately leaps to
his death.

Churning way beneath the surface of the novel's narrative is
a fantastically rich and engaging mythic and folkloristic universe. Further, this universe is introduced to us through the
music of Louis Armstrong, whose music then forms the overall
structure for the novel. If that is the case, the subsequent
narrative and all of the action which follows can be read as one
long blues solo. Critic Albert Murray, a close associate of
Ellison's, put it this way:

> *Invisible Man* was *par excellence* the literary ex-
> tension of the blues. Ellison had taken an everyday
> twelve-bar blues tune (by a man from down South
> sitting in a manhole up North in New York, singing
> and signifying about how he got there) and scored it
> for full orchestra. This was indeed something differ-
> ent and something more than run-of-the-mill U.S.
> fiction. It had new dimensions of rhetorical resonance
> (based on lying and signifying). It employed a startlingly
> effective fusion of narrating realism and surrealism,
> and it achieved a unique but compelling combination
> of the naturalistic, the ridiculous, and the downright
> hallucinatory. (*Omni-Americans*, 167)

What is important about Murray's observation here is that it isolates, in *Invisible Man,* a unique aesthetic. There has been much talk of late about a "black aesthetic," but there has been, fundamentally, a failure to examine those elements of the black experience in America which could genuinely constitute an aesthetic. With no real knowledge of folk culture—blues, folk songs, folk narratives, spirituals, dance styles, gospels, speech, and oral history—there is very little possibility that a black aesthetic will be realized in our literature.

Ellison, however, finds the aesthetic all around him. He finds it in memories of Oklahoma background. He finds it in preachers, blues singers, hustlers, gamblers, jazzmen, boxers, dancers, and itinerant storytellers. He notes carefully the subtleties of American speech patterns. He pulls the covers off the stereotypes in order to probe beneath the surface where the hard-core mythic truth lies. He keeps checking out style. The way people walk, what they say, and what they leave *unsaid.* If anyone has been concerned with a "black aesthetic" it has certainly got to be Ralph Ellison. And even if you disagree with Ellison's political thrust these days, you have to dig his consistent concern for capturing the essential truths of the black man's experience in America.

And where are these essential truths embodied, if not in the folk culture? Do not Stackolee, High John the Conqueror, John Henry, Shine, and the Signifying Monkey reveal vital aspects of our group experience? Or has the current "rediscovery" of African culture obscured the fact that however disruptive slavery must have been to our original African personalities, our fathers and mothers intuitively understood what aspect of it could be rescued and reshaped? And did not this reshaping indicate a *willed* desire to survive and maintain one's own specific outlook on life? Didn't it exhibit a willed desire to survive in the face of danger? What kind of people were they in their weaknesses and their strengths? Haven't we read their slave narratives and listened carefully to their songs? And hasn't the essential spirit that they breathed into these expressions continued to manifest itself in all meaningful aspects of our struggle? We must address ourselves to this kind of humanity because it is meaningful and within our immediate reach. To do so means understanding something essential about the persistence of tradition, understanding the manner in which values are shaped out of tradition, and—what's more important—understanding the values whose fundamental function was to bind us together into a community of shared feelings and memories in order that we might survive.

Ellison's protagonist, when confronted with possible expulsion from his Southern Negro college, suffers deeply at the thought of losing his regional roots. In his longing for a sustainable image of the world that has created him, he transforms an "ordinary" housemother into a ritual goddess. Dig. Here is your black aesthetic at its best:

> *Ha! To the gray-haired matron in the final row. Ha! Miss Susie, Miss Susie Gresham, back there looking at that co-ed smiling at that he-ed—listen to me, the bungling bugler of words, imitating the trumpet and the trombone's timbre, playing thematic variations like a baritone horn. Hey! old connoisseur of voice sounds, of voices without messages, of newsless winds, listen to the vowel sounds and the crackling dentals, to the low harsh gutturals of empty anguish, now riding the curve of a preacher's rhythm I heard long ago in a Baptist church, stripped now of its imagery: No suns having hemorrhages, no moons weeping tears, no earthworms refusing the sacred flesh and dancing in the earth on Easter morn. Ha! singing achievement. Ha! booming success, intoning. Ha! acceptance, Ha! a river of word-sounds filled with drowned passions, floating, Ha! floating, Ha! with wrecks of unachievable ambitions and stillborn revolts, sweeping their ears, Ha! ranged stiff before me, necks stretched forward with listening ears, Ha! a-spraying the ceiling and a-drumming the dark-stained after rafter, that seasoned crossarm of torturous timber mellowed in the kiln of a thousand voices; playing, Ha! as upon a xylophone; words marching like the student band, up the campus and down again, blaring triumphant sounds empty of triumphs. Hey, Miss Susie! the sound of words that were no words, counterfeit notes singing achievements yet unachieved, riding upon the wings of my voice out to you, old matron, who knew the voice*

> *sounds of the Founder and knew the accents and*
> *echo of his promise; your gray old head cocked with*
> *the young around you, your eyes closed, face ec-*
> *static, as I toss the word-sounds in my breath, my*
> *bellows, my fountain, like bright-colored balls in a*
> *water spout—hear me, old matron, justify now this*
> *sound with your dear old nod of affirmation, your*
> *closed-eye smile and bow of recognition, who'll never*
> *be fooled with the mere content of words, not my*
> *words, not these pinfeathered flighters that stroke your*
> *lids till they flutter with ecstasy with but the mere*
> *echoed noise of the promise. And after the singing and*
> *outward marching, you seize my hand and sing out*
> *quavering, "Boy, some day you'll make the Founder*
> *proud!" Ha! Susie Gresham, Mother Gresham, guardian*
> *of the hot young women on the puritan benches who*
> *couldn't see your Jordan's water for their private*
> *steam; you, relic of slavery whom the campus loved*
> *but did not understand, aged, of slavery, yet bearer of*
> *something warm and vital and all-enduring, of which*
> *in that island of shame we were not ashamed—it was to*
> *you on the final row I directed my rush of sound, and*
> *it was you of whom I thought with shame and regret*
> *as I waited for the ceremony to begin. (IM, 88–89)*

This poetic narrative is the prelude to the ceremony in which Rev. Homer Barbee, taking the role of tribal poet, ritually consecrates the memory of the Founder. His speech is permeated with myth. The Founder's image is not merely locked into legitimate history, it bobs and weaves between facts, half-remembered truths, and apocrypha. The Founder is perceived by Barbee as a culture hero bringing order out of chaos, bringing wisdom to bear upon fear and ignorance. He is compared to Moses, Aristotle, and Jesus. He is called by Homer Barbee "prophet," "godly man," "the great spirit," and "the great sun." In his hardships and moments of danger, he is helped by strange emissaries, one of whom, Barbee says, may have come "direct from above." Another of the Founder's helpers is an old slave who is ridiculed by the town's children:

> He, the old slave, showing a surprising knowledge of
> such matters—*germology* and *scabology*—ha! ha!

ha!—he called it, and what youthful skill of the hands!
For he shaved our skull, and cleansed our wound
and bound it neat with bandages stolen from the
home of an unsuspecting leader of the mob, ha! (*IM*,
94)

Barbee makes his audience, composed primarily of black college students, identify with the Founder. No, in fact, under
the spell of the ritual sermon, they must *become* the Founder.
They must don the mask of the god, so to speak. All of these
details are said to be remembered by the students, yet Barbee
has a compulsive need to reiterate them, to recharge them
with meaning by reconsecrating them. His essential role, as
ritual priest, is to keep before them the "painful details" of the
Founder's life. These are memories that his young audience
must internalize, and share fully, if they are to ever realize
themselves in the passage from adolescence into maturity. And
this is the function of folk culture. This is what Ellison sensed
in the blues. In an essay entitled "Richard Wright's Blues," he
notes:

> The blues is an impulse to keep the painful details
> and episodes of a brutal experience alive in one's
> aching consciousness, to finger its jagged grain, and
> to transcend it, not by the consolation of philosophy
> but by squeezing from it a near-tragic, near-comic
> lyricism. As a form, the blues is an autobiographical
> chronicle of personal catastrophe expressed lyrically.
> (*S&A*, 78–79)

In "Blues People," a review of Imamu Baraka's (LeRoi Jones's)
book, he makes this statement about the role of the blues
singer:

> Bessie Smith might have been a "blues queen" to
> the society at large, but within the tighter Negro
> community where the blues were part of the total
> way of life, and a major expression of an attitude
> toward life, she was a priestess, a celebrant who
> affirmed the values of the group and man's ability to
> deal with chaos.[6]

Blues represent a central creative motif throughout *Invisible Man* from the hero's "descent" into the music at the beginning of the novel. The blues allow Trueblood to face up to himself after the disastrous event of making his daughter pregnant. The blues inform the texture of much of the novel's prose:

> My stomach felt raw. From somewhere across the quiet of the campus the sound of guitar-blues plucked from an out-of-tune piano drifted towards me like a lazy, shimmering wave, like the echoed whistle of a lonely train, and my head went over again, against a tree, and I could hear it splattering the flowering vines. (*IM*, 122)

And at another point the hero contemplates the meaning of this blues lyric:

> *She's got feet like a monkey*
> *Legs*
> *Legs, Legs like a maaad*
> *Bulldog.*
> (*IM*, 134)

"What does it mean?" he thinks.

> And why describe anyone in such contradictory words? Was it a sphinx? Did old Chaplin-pants, old dusty-butt, lover her or hate her; or was he merely singing? What kind of woman could love a dirty fellow like that, anyway? And how could even *he* love her if she were as respulsive as the song described? . . . I strode along, hearing the cartman's song become a lonesome, broad-toned whistle now that flowered at the end of each phrase into a tremulous, blue-toned chord. And in its flutter and swoop, I heard the sound of a railroad train highballing it, lonely across the lonely night. He was the Devil's son-in-law, all right, and he was a man who could whistle a three-toned chord. . . . God damn, I thought, they're a hell of a people! And I didn't know whether it was pride or disgust that suddenly flashed over me. (*IM*, 134–35)

Why this emphasis on folklore and blues culture? In a recent issue of the *College Language Association* (CLA) *Journal,* George Kent supplies an answer which many of those who consider themselves nationalists should well consider:

> Offering the first drawings of a group's character, preserving situations repeated in the history of the group, describing the boundaries of thought and feeling, projecting the group's wisdom in symbols expressing its will to survive, embodying those values by which it lives and dies, folklore seemed, as Ellison described it, basic to the portrayal of the essential spirit of black people.[7]

Ellison's spiritual roots are, therefore, deep in the black American folk tradition. I think that this awareness of specifically black contributions to the so-called mainstream of American life gives him a fundamental certainty that no matter how much he praises the writers of the white West, he is still himself: Ralph *Waldo* Ellison. Much of Ellison's concern with the major literary figures of Europe and America emanates from his sincere belief that it is the duty of every writer, black or white, to be fully aware of the best that has ever been written. For Ellison that has never meant *becoming* a white man. It meant bringing to bear on literature and language the force of one's own sensibility and modes of feeling. It meant learning the craft of fiction, even from white artists, but dominating that craft so much that you don't play like the other feller anymore. That trumpet you got in your hand may have been made in Germany, but you sure sound like my Uncle Rufus whooping his coming-home call across the cotton fields. But you got to master the instrument first, Ellison might say. I would agree to that, but add this: you got to somehow master *yourself* in the process.

If there is any fundamental difference I have with Ellison, it is his, perhaps unintentional, tendency to imply that black writers should confine their range of cultural inquiry strictly to American—and European—subject matter. For a man who was not exactly parochial about his search for knowledge to subtly impose such attitudes on young writers is to deny the best aspects of his own development as an artist.

Young writers, on the other hand, should not fall for any specious form of reasoning that limits the range of their inquiry strictly to African and Afro-American subject matter. A realistic movement among the black arts community should be about the *extension* of the *remembered* and a *resurrection* of the *unremembered*; should be about an engagement with the *selves* we know and the *selves* we have forgotten. Finally, it should be about a synthesis of the conglomerate of world knowledge; all that is meaningful and moral and that makes one stronger and wiser, in order to live as fully as possible as a human being. What will make this knowledge ours is what we do with it, how we color it to suit our specific needs. Its value to us will depend upon what we bring to bear upon it. In our dispersal, we can "dominate" Western culture or be "dominated" by it. It all depends on what you feel about yourself. Any black writer or politician who does not believe that black people have created something powerful and morally sustaining in their four hundred or so years here has declared himself a loser before the war begins. How would we create, even fight, denying the total weight of our particular historical experience *here* in America.

I must emphasize the word "total" because, as Ellison and Albert Murray often explain, there is a tendency among American sociologists and black creative intellectuals to perceive our history in purely pathological terms. For example, Don L. Lee makes a statement in *Ebony* magazine to the following effect: If you don't know about rats and roaches, you don't know about the black experience. Why define yourself in purely negative terms, when you know that your very life, in its most profound aspects, is not merely a result of the negative? We are not simply, in *all* areas of our sensibilities, merely a set of black reactions to white oppression. And neither should our art be merely an aesthetic reaction to white art. It has finally got to exist as good art also because, in terms of the development of a national art, excellent art is, in and of itself, the best propaganda you can have. By now, we should be free enough to use any viable techniques that will allow us to shape an art that breathes and is based essentially on our own emotional and cultural imperatives.

Ellison, however, almost overwhelmingly locates his cultural, philosphical, and literary sensibility in the West. That's his prerogative, and that prerogative should be protected. But being so-called free individuals, at least on the question of whom one accepts as "literary ancestors," it is possible to extend one's vocabulary and memory in any manner one chooses. It's already being done in music; Coltrane, Sun Ra, Pharoah Sanders, and Leon Thomas indicate devices, procedures, functions, attitudes, and concerns that are not vividly indicated in Euro-American culture. They indicate a synthesis and a rejection of Western musical theory at the same time, just as aspects of Louis Armstrong's trumpet playing indicated, in its time, a respect for the traditional uses of the instrument on the one hand, and on the other, to the squares, it indicated a "gross defilement" of the instrument. I recall once reading an article about a son of A. J. Sax, the Belgian instrument maker, who said something to the effect that he didn't believe his father intended for the instrument to be played the way jazz musicians were playing it. Yeah, you can take the other dude's instruments and play like your Uncle Rufus's hog callings. But there is another possibility also: *You could make your own instrument.* And if you can sing through that instrument, you can impose your voice on the world in a heretofore-unthought-of manner.

In short, you can create another world view, another cosmology springing from your own specific grounds, but transcending them as your new world realizes itself.

All black creative artists owe Ellison special gratitude. He and a few others of his generation have struggled to keep the culture alive in their artistic works. We should not be content with merely basking in the glow of their works. We need what they have given us. But the world has changed. Which is as it should be. And we have changed in the world. Which is quite natural. Because everybody and everything is change. However, what Ellison teaches us is that it is not possible to move toward meaningful creative ends without somehow taking with you the accumulated weight of your forebears' experiences.

What I think we have to do is to understand our roles as synthesizers: the creators of new and exciting visions out of the accumulated weight of our Western experience. We must also deeply understand the specific reasons, both historically and

emotionally, that cause many of us to *feel* that there is a range
of ideas beyond those strictly of the West. To be more precise,
no philosophical, political, or religious attitude in the world
today. Western or Eastern, fully provides the means of mankind's spiritual and psychic liberation. No one system of ethics,
oriental or occidental, exists in harmony with the social world
from which it springs. Why?

Perhaps it is because the one central component of man's
sensibility that would allow him to survive on human terms has
never been allowed to flower. And that is the artistic sensibility
that essentially defines man as a spiritual being in the world.
That is because politicians have never accepted the idea that
art was simply a public gesture, hence not political. Therefore,
Ellison is incorrect when he says to Irving Howe: "I would
have said that it [the novel] is always a public gesture, though
not necessarily a political one." This statement is only half-
true. The novel is *both* a public gesture *and* a political gesture.
As Ellison knows, burning a Cadillac on the White House
lawn[8] is a public gesture, but it is amusingly political also. The
minute a work of art enters the social sphere, it faces the
problem of being preceived on all kinds of levels, from the
grossly political to the philosophically sublime. It just be's that
way, that's all. And Marx hasn't a thing to do with it. But
Marxists implicitly understand the relationship between a work's
public character and its political character, however minute a
work's political characteristics might be. And that is why totali-
tarian and fascist regimes must suppress all genuine art. "Who
is that fool babbling all kinds of ghosts and chimera out of his
eyes, ears, hands, feet, and mouth? We can't understand him.
He must certainly be enemy."

In a system of strategies, of statement, and counterstate-
ment, art is just one other element in the ring, even when it
dons an elaborate mask and pretends not to be saying what it
really says. *Invisible Man* is artistically one of the world's
greatest novels; it is also one of the world's most successful
"political" novels. It is just that Ellison's politics are ritualistic
as opposed to secular. Ellison's manipulation of rhetorical imagery in *Invisible Man* is enough to blow the average politician
off the stand.

The poet, the writer, is a key bearer of culture. Through

myth, he is the manipulator of both the collective conscious and unconscious. If he is good, he is the master of rhetorical imagery. And, as such, he is much more physically powerful than the secular politician. And that is why he is, to some extent, in some societies, feared and suppressed by secular politicians. Sometimes, he is suppressed even by the laity who must finally embrace his art, if it is to live. But the suppression of art, whether it occurs in the West or in the East, whether it occurs under capitalism or socialism, is detrimental to man's spiritual survival. Without spirit, the substance of all his material accomplishments means essentially nothing. Therefore, what we might consider is a system of politics and art that is as fluid, as functional, and as expansive as black music. No such system now exists; we're gonna have to build it. And when it is finally realized, it will be a conglomerate, gleaned from the *whole* of all our experiences.

Later now:
A cool *asante*
in the hey y'all,
habari gani to yo' mamma,
this has been your sweet Poppa Stoppa
running the voodoo down.

NOTES

1. Ralph Ellison, "The World and the Jug," in *Shadow and Act* (New York: Random House, 1964). Quotations from this essay and others in *Shadow and Act* are cited in the text as *S&A*.
2. John O Killens, *Freedom*, June 1952, 7. Killen's comments are reprinted in Harold Cruse, *The Crisis of the Negro Intellectual* (New York: William Morrow & Co., 1967), 235.
3. See Maulana Karenga's seven criteria for culture in *The Quotable Karenga* (US), 1967. Note that Maulana makes mythology one of the seven criteria for culture, and creative motif another important one. See also Cruse, *Crisis of the Negro Intellectual*.
4. Ralph Ellison, *Invisible Man* (New York: Random House, 1952), 332–33. Subsequent references are cited in the text as *IM*.
5. For example, Sam Greenlee's novel *The Spook Who Sat by the Door* (New York: R. W. Baron, 1969) is an atrocious novel. It lacks style and conscious sense of craft. It is clearly more of a "manual" than a "revolutionary" novel. Its major premise is excellent, but flawed by Greenlee's inability to bring it off. Its "revolutionary content" is never firmly rooted

in a form that is sustaining below the mere surface of graphic detail. Where Greenlee could have written a "great" novel, one both excellently written and revolutionary in stance, he blew the challenge by a glib adherence to militancy.

6. Ellison's review of *Blues People* (*Shadow and Act*, 257) is stringently critical, and at times a little beside the point. What he really seems to be doing here is castigating LeRoi Jones for not writing the book that he (Ellison) would have written. The specific thrust of *Blues People* was never really analyzed. Of course Ellison is capable of analyzing the specific ideas in *Blues People*, but he just wanted to write his own essay on the blues. And his essay is worthwhile and meaningful, too.

7. See George E. Kent, "Ralph Ellison and Afro-American Folk and Cultural Tradition," *College Language Association* (CLA) *Journal* 13 (1970): 256–76.

8. See Ellison's short story "It Always Breaks Out," *Partisan Review*, Spring 1963: 13–28.

The Black Writer's Role, III
James Baldwin

This is the third article in a series on the role of the black writer. We have previously discussed Richard Wright and Ralph Ellison in terms of particular historical and social problems confronting Afro-American writers. What we have been trying to arrive at is some kind of synthesis of the writer's function as an oppressed individual and a creative artist.

It was Baldwin who attempted a reevaluation of the status of American "protest novel." The attempt has opened him to much criticism. Most of it stemming from Baldwin's failure to arrive at a more deeply considered idea of the American novel; and further his failure to utilize the "Negro tradition" to its fullest extent. Sylvester Leaks accuses him of having "studied too much English and not enough people—especially Black people."

In *Anger, and Beyond,* a collection of essays and interviews on the black writer [edited by Herbert Hill], Albert Murray states that Baldwin's work is now characterized by the same sense of protest that Baldwin accused Wright of in the essay entitled "Everybody's Protest Novel."

There is a certain amount of truth in both of these charges. I personally find it difficult to ascribe any particular set of artistic values to Baldwin. Simply, because he is a very complex person. His work and his friends testify to the truth of this statement. Looking over Baldwin's life since about 1948, one is confronted with a personality that is constantly grappling with problems; constantly tearing himself and the world apart in order to discover some essential truth. The most striking thing about this search is its public character. It is as if the public were witnessing something on the order of a confession; and the only thing that finally saves it from being something so mundane is the excellence of the writing. His work is suffused with a incisive sense of self-pity. But it never remains simply that. It never fails to engage our attention, even when it is unsuccessful, the way *Another Country* is unsuccessful. One always senses behind the words a personality that is grappling with a large dirty world that it does not understand. A world, best described by the word *conundrum*, a word which pops up often in his essays.

He knows that the white world offers no simple solutions to these conundrums, these riddles; but he hacks away at them like a black Job grappling with a mystery that is ultimately larger than any one man's life. And because he has been greatly concerned with identity, much of Baldwin's analysis of the world involves, in essence, an analysis of himself.

Baldwin, more so than Wright or Ellison, has been extremely preoccupied with identity—his identity as a black man and as an American writer. I stress American because along with his "Negro-ness" it is his sense of being an American that finally emerges as a central aspect of Baldwin's vision of himself:

> In my necessity to find the terms on which my experience could be related to that of others, Negroes and whites, writers and non-writers, I proved to my astonishment, to be as American as any Texas G.I. And I found my experience was shared by every American writer I knew in Paris. Like me, they had been divorced from their origins, and it turned out to make very little difference that the origins of white Americans were European and mine were African— they were no more at home in Europe than I was.

And by extention of that identity, the Negro is viewed as an American phenomena:

> The story of the Negro in America is the story of America—or more precisely, it is the story of Americans. . . . The Negro in America, gloomily referred to as that shadow which lies athwart our national life.

In elaborating upon these points, Baldwin illustrates that the price which America must pay for the dehumanization of the black man is her own dehumanization; and further, the destruction of the black man's identity is the destruction of the identity of America. Mixed up in all of this is what he calls a "fruitless tension between traditional master and slave." Baldwin believes that this tension has nothing to do with reality.

I believe that it has everything to do with reality, however bizarre that reality may seem. Baldwin has a penchant for allowing himself to fall into a few vague idealistic traps. Mostly, it is because he is sensitive enough to see through to the horror but is unable to confront it. At least real confrontation with that must be in his eyes, an existential oppression, is constantly being sidestepped.

Baldwin usually ends up begging out, or by falling back on a kind of supernormal kind of "love." This happens in *The Fire Next Time* where he warns America of her impending doom for her sins against black people. In his novel *Another Country,* the characters seem to exist outside of a social context; and the choices that they make are essentially unimportant. His play *Blues for Mister Charlie* ends with a preacher taking up the Bible and the gun. It is as if the author cannot decide what exactly he wants his characters to do or to be. And it is this duality that is finally the most disconcerting thing about much of Baldwin's work, even the best of it.

Much of what he had to say about America, and the Black man's relation to her, was extremely timely. And, I suppose, that much of it had to be said the way Baldwin said it. That is, it had to offer alternatives which white America, if it were humane, could accept. Once having had a writer like Baldwin lay bare the corrupt morality of America, and in so complete and thorough a manner, a way was paved for another dynamic—a new force was unleased among younger black writers, which had as its purpose an internal dialogue among black people. Baldwin's impassioned essays and shrill outcries were directed primarily at white America. Hence, he joined the tradition of pleading with white America for the humanity of the Negro; instead of addressing himself to black people and their problems.

Baldwin's popularity coincided with the "civil rights revolution." And in terms of the character of the civil rights movement, his work represents both the moral substance of the movement, and its ultimate sterility. Baldwin's love-centeredness springs from the same sources fundamentally as Reverend King's, whose relationship to certain social forces, forced him to understand that he must take a position vis-à-vis those forces. Baldwin did just that. And in doing so, confused and enlightened many Black writers at the same time.

Confusion because he, or few other writers, have asked themselves: What is supposed to be the function of literature in this society in the first place? Baldwin has asserted that the writer is supposed to be committed to "truth." Whose truth—the oppressed or the oppressor's—he does not say. What we are left with is a body of literature which has no focus. Also, there is no attempt at a synthesis which supports the writer's aesthetic and political impulses. Using Baldwin as a working example, it is clear that there is a certain amount of tension underlying these problems.

But, Baldwin acting as the conscience of the civil rights movement comes closer than any writer before him to an essential aspect of the problem. And that is commitment to some kind of social dynamic. Here is where Ellison's priestly ritual role takes on, what I believe to be, a more significant meaning. The writer must somehow place himself at the center of the community's cultural and political activity and perform the role as interpreter of the mysteries of life. He must resist and submit, at once, to the day-to-day demands of the community.

Out of this creative tension between the individual and the collective will emerge a synthesis appropriate to the revolutionary demands of the situation. For most black writers to engage in this kind of confrontation with themselves and their people, they must rid themselves of certain middle-class hang-ups about the value of their art to the larger society, i.e., white America; and pledge themselves to the psychological liberation of black people. All of this must be done while pursuing whatever petty offers the creative establishment makes to aspiring writers.

Baldwin's problem was that he was the conscience of a movement (civil rights) which has as its goal integration into a dying system, instead of the destruction of the white idea of the world. In *The Fire Next Time,* he begins to understand certain very basic things about black people in this society, the most important of which is that the only thing whites have that black people should want is power. Further, black people, because of the manner in which they are situated within this society, have the means of destroying the American dream. However, these are still the observations of a man who fundamentally wants to "save" America.

James Baldwin is the articulate spokesman of that wing of the Negro establishment which sees America's race problem as simply a moral question. I suggest that Baldwin performed an important service to black America by exposing white America's total lack of conscience. If she could ignore as impassioned a cry as Baldwin's then she was beyond saving.

As a "spokesman" for an oppressed people, Baldwin met with mixed success. As a writer for these same people, Baldwin has missed the point by a wide margin. His uncertainty over identity and his failure to utilize, to its fullest extent, traditional aspects of Afro-American culture has tended to dull the intensity of his work. Therefore, we are still awaiting a writer totally committed to the destiny of black people, a writer who has decided to explore in the most creative fashion possible all aspects of the Afro-American presence in the United States.

1966

The Black Arts Movement

The Black Arts Movement is radically opposed to any concept of the artist that alienates him from his community. This movement is the aesthetic and spiritual sister of the Black Power concept. As such, it envisions an art that speaks directly to the needs and aspirations of black America. In order to perform this task, the Black Arts Movement proposes a radical reordering of the Western cultural aesthetic. It proposes a separate symbolism, mythology, critique, and iconology. The Black Arts and the Black Power concepts both relate broadly to the Afro-American's desire for self-determination and nationhood. Both concepts are nationalistic. One is concerned with the relationship between art and politics; the other with the art of politics.

Recently, these two movements have begun to merge: the political values inherent in the Black Power concept are now finding concrete expression in the aesthetics of Afro-American dramatists, poets, choreographers, musicians, and novelists. A main tenet of Black Power is the necessity for black people to define the world in their own terms. The black artist has made the same point in the context of aesthetics. The two movements postulate that there are in fact and in spirit two Americas— one black, one white. The black artist takes this to mean that his primary duty is to speak to the spiritual and cultural needs of black people. Therefore, the main thrust of this new breed of contemporary writers is to confront the contradictions arising out of the black man's experience in the racist West. Currently, these writers are reevaluating Western aesthetics, the

62

traditional role of the writer, and the social function of art. Implicit in this reevaluation is the need to develop a "black aesthetic." It is the opinion of many black writers, I among them, that the Western aesthetic has run its course: it is impossible to construct anything meaningful within its decaying structure. We advocate a cultural revolution in art and ideas. The cultural values inherent in Western history must either be radicalized or destroyed, and we will probably find that even radicalization is impossible. In fact, what is needed is a whole new system of ideas. Poet Don L. Lee expresses it:

> We must destroy Faulkner, dick, jane, and other perpetuators of evil. It's time for DuBois, Nat Turner, and Kwame Nkrumah. As Frantz Fanon points out: destroy the culture and you destroy the people. This must not happen. Black artists are culture stabilizers; bringing back old values, and introducing new ones. Black art will talk to the people and with the will of the people stop impending "protective custody."

The Black Arts Movement eschews "protest" literature. It speaks directly to black people. Implicit in the concept of "protest" literature, as Brother Etheridge Knight has made clear, is an appeal to white morality:

> Now any Black man who masters the technique of his particular art form, who adheres to the white aesthetic, and who directs his work towards a white audience is, in one sense, protesting. And implicit in the act of protest is the belief that a change will be forthcoming once the masters are aware of the protestor's "grievance" (the very word connotes begging, supplications to the gods). Only when that belief has faded and protestings end, will Black art begin.

Brother Knight also has some interesting statements about the development of a "black aesthetic":

> Unless the Black artist establishes a "Black aesthetic" he will have no future at all. To accept the white aesthetic is to accept and validate a society that will

not allow him to live. The Black artist must create
new forms and new values, sing new songs (or purify
old ones); and along with other Black authorities, he
must create a new history, new symbols, myths and
legends (and purify old ones by fire). And the Black
artist, in creating his own aesthetic, must be account-
able for it only to the Black people. Further, he must
hasten his own disolution as an individual (in the
Western sense)—painful though, the process may
be, having been breast-fed the poison of "individual
experience."

When we speak of a "black aesthetic" several things are
meant. First, we assume that there is already in existence the
basis for such an aesthetic. Essentially, it consists of an African-
American cultural tradition. But this aesthetic is finally, by
implication, broader than that tradition. It encompasses most
of the usable elements of Third World culture. The motive
behind the black aesthetic is the destruction of the white thing,
the destruction of white ideas, and white ways of looking at the
world. The new aesthetic is mostly predicated on an ethics
which asks the question: Whose vision of the world is finally
more meaningful, ours or the white oppressors? What is truth?
Or more precisely, whose truth shall we express, that of the
oppressed or of the oppressors? These are basic questions.
Black intellectuals of previous decades failed to ask them.
Further, national and international affairs demand that we ap-
praise the world in terms of our own interests. It is clear that
the question of human survival is at the core of contemporary
experience. The black artist must address himself to this reality
in the strongest terms possible. In a context of world upheaval,
ethics and aesthetics must interact positively and be consistent
with the demands for a more spiritual world. Consequently,
the Black Arts Movement is an ethical movement. Ethical, that
is, from the viewpoint of the oppressed. And much of the
oppression confronting the Third World and black America is
directly traceable to the Euro-American cultural sensibility.
This sensibility, antihuman in nature, has, until recently, dominated the psyches of most black artists and intellectuals. It

must be destroyed before the black creative artist can have a meaningful role in the transformation of society.

It is this natural reaction to an alien sensibility that informs the cultural attitudes of the Black Arts and the Black Power movements. It is a profound ethical sense that makes a black artist question a society in which art is one thing and the actions of men another. The Black Arts Movement believes that your ethics and your aesthetics are one. That the contradictions between ethics and aesthetics in Western society is symptomatic of a dying culture.

The term "Black Arts" is of ancient origin, but it was first used in a positive sense by LeRoi Jones:

> We are unfair
> And unfair
> We are black magicians
> Black arts we make
> in black labs of the heart
>
> The fair are fair
> and deathly white
>
> The day will not save them
> And we own the night

There is also a section of the poem "Black Dada Nihilismus" that carries the same motif. But a fuller amplification of the nature of the new aesthetics appears in the poem "Black Art":

> Poems are bullshit unless they are
> teeth or trees or lemons piled
> on a step. Or black ladies dying
> of men leaving nickel hearts
> beating them down. Fuck poems
> and they are useful, they shoot
> come at you, love what you are,
> breathe like wrestlers, or shudder
> strangely after pissing. We want live
> words of the hip world, live flesh &
> coursing blood. Hearts Brains
> Souls splintering fire. We want poems

> like fists beating niggers out of Jocks
> or dagger poems in the slimy bellies
> of the owner-jews . . .

Poetry is a concrete function, an action. No more abstractions. Poems are physical entities: fists, daggers, airplane poems, and poems that shoot guns. Poems are transformed from physical object into personal forces:

> Put it on him poem. Strip him naked
> to the world. Another bad poem cracking
> steel knuckles in a jewlady's mouth
> Poem scream poison gas on breasts in green berets . . .

Then the poem affirms the integral relationship between black art and black people:

> Let Black people understand
> that they are the lovers and the sons
> of lovers and warriors and sons
> of warriors Are poems & poets &
> all the loveliness here in the world

It ends with the following lines, a central assertion in both the Black Arts Movement and the philosophy of Black Power:

> We want a black poem. And a
> Black World.
> Let the world be a Black Poem
> And Let All Black People Speak This Poem
> Silently
> Or LOUD

The poem comes to stand for the collective consciousness and unconscious of black America—the real impulse in back of the Black Power movement, which is the will toward self-determination and nationhood, a radical reordering of the nature and function of both art and the artist.

2.

In the spring of 1964, LeRoi Jones, Charles Patterson, William Patterson, Clarence Reed, Johnny Moore, and a number of other black artists opened the Black Arts Repertory Theater School. They produced a number of plays including Jones's *Experimental Death Unit #1, Black Mass, Jello,* and *Dutchman*. They also initiated a series of poetry readings and concerts. These activities represented the most advanced tendencies in the movement and were of excellent artistic quality. The Black Arts school came under immediate attack by the New York power structure. The Establishment, fearing black creativity, did exactly what it was expected to do—it attacked the theater and all of its values. In the meantime, the school was granted funds by OEO through HARYOU-ACT. Lacking a cultural program itself, HARYOU turned to the only organization which addressed itself to the needs of the community. In keeping with its "revolutionary" cultural ideas, the Black Arts Theater took its programs into the streets of Harlem. For three months, the theater presented plays, concerts, and poetry readings to the people of the community. Plays that shattered the illusions of the American body politic, and awakened black people to the meaning of their lives.

Then the hawks from the OEO moved in and chopped off the funds. Again, this should have been expected. The Black Arts Theater stood in radical opposition to the feeble attitudes about culture of the "War On Poverty" bureaucrats. And later, because of internal problems, the theater was forced to close. But the Black Arts group proved that the community could be served by a valid and dynamic art. It also proved that there was a definite need for a cultural revolution in the black community.

With the closing of the Black Arts Theater, the implications of what Brother Jones and his colleagues were trying to do took on even more significance. Black Arts groups sprang up on the West Coast and the idea spread to Detroit, Philadelphia, Jersey City, New Orleans, and Washington D.C. Black Arts movements began on the campuses of San Francisco Stage College, Fisk University, Lincoln University, Hunter College in the Bronx, Columbia University, and Oberlin College. In Watts, after the rebellion, Maulana Karenga welded the Blacks Arts

Movement into a cohesive cultural ideology which owed much to the work of LeRoi Jones. Karenga sees culture as the most important element in the struggle for self-determination:

> Culture is the basis of all ideas, images and ac-
> tions. To move is to move culturally, i.e., by a set of
> values given to you by your culture.
>   Without a culture Negroes are only a set of reac-
> tions to white people.
>   The seven criteria for culture are:
>   1. Mythology
>   2. History
>   3. Social Organization
>   4. Political Organization
>   5. Economic Organization
>   6. Creative Motif
>   7. Ethos

In drama, LeRoi Jones represents the most advanced aspects of the movement. He is its prime mover and chief designer. In a poetic essay entitled "The Revolutionary Theatre," he out-lines the iconology of the movement:

> The Revolutionary Theatre should force change: it
> should be change. (All their faces turned into the
> lights and you work on them black nigger magic, and
> cleanse them at having seen the ugliness. And if the
> beautiful see themselves, they will love themselves.)
> We are preaching virtue again, but by that to mean
> NOW, toward what seems the most constructive use
> of the word.

The theater that Jones proposes is inextricably linked to the Afro-American political dynamic. And such a link is perfectly consistent with Black America's contemporary demands. For theatre is potentially the most social of all the arts. It is an integral part of the socializing process. It exists in direct rela-tionship to the audience it claims to serve. The decadence and inanity of the contemporary American theater is an accurate reflection of the state of American society. Albee's *Who's Afraid of Virginia Woolf?* is very American: sick white lives in a homosexual hell hole. The theater of white America is escapist, refusing to confront concrete reality. Into this cultural emptiness come the musicals, an up-tempo version of the same stale lives. And the use of Negroes in such plays as *Hello, Dolly!* and *Hallelujah Baby* does not alert their nature; it compounds the problem. These plays are simply hipper versions of the minstrel show. They present Negroes acting out the hang-ups of middle-class white America. Consequently, the American theater is a palliative prescribed to bourgeois patients who refuse to see the world as it is. Or, more crucially, as the world sees them. It is no accident, therefore, that the most "important" plays come from Europe—Brecht, Weiss, and Ghelderode. And even these have begun to run dry.

The Black Arts Theater, the theater of LeRoi Jones, is a radical alternative to the sterility of the American theater. It is primarily a theater of the spirit, confronting the black man in his interaction with his brothers and with the white thing.

> Our theater will show victims so that their brothers in the audience will be better able to understand that they are the brothers of victims, and that they themselves are blood brothers. And what we show must cause the blood to rush, so that prerevolutionary temperaments will be bathed in this blood, and it will cause their deepest souls to move, and they will find themselves tensed and clenched, even ready to die, at what the soul has been taught. We will scream and cry, murder, run through the streets in agony, if it means some soul will be moved, moved to actual life understanding of what the world is, and what it ought to be. We are preaching virtue and feeling, and a natural sense of the self in the world. All men live in the world, and the world ought to be a place for them to live.

The victims in the world of Jones's early plays are Clay, murdered by the white bitch-goddess in *Dutchman*, and Walker Vessels, the revolutionary in *The Slave*. Both of these plays present black men in transition. Clay, the middle-class Negro trying to get himself a little action from Lula, digs himself and his own truth only to get murdered after telling her like it really is:

Just let me bleed you, you loud whore, and one poem vanished. A whole people neurotics, struggling to keep from being sane. And the only thing that would cure the neurosis would be your murder. Simple as that. I mean if I murdered you, then other white people would understand me. You understand? No, I guess not. If Bessie Smith had killed some white people she wouldn't needed that music. She could have talked very straight and plain about the world. Just straight two and two are four. Money. Power. Luxury. Like that. All of them. Crazy niggers turning their back on sanity. When all it needs is that simple act. Just murder. Would make us all sane.

But Lula understands, and she kills Clay first. In a perverse way it is Clay's nascent knowledge of himself that threatens the existence of Lula's idea of the world. Symbolically, and in fact, the relationship between Clay (black America) and Lula (white America) is rooted in the historical castration of black manhood. And in the twisted psyche of white America, the black man is both an object of love and hate. Analogous attitudes exist in most black Americans, but for decidedly different reasons. Clay is doomed when he allows himself to participate in Lula's "fantasy" in the first place. It is the fantasy to which Frantz Fanon alludes in *The Wretched of the Earth* and *Black Skins, White Mask:* the native's belief that he can acquire the oppressor's power by acquiring his symbols, one of which is the white woman. When Clay finally digs himself it it too late.

Walker Vessels, in *The Slave,* is Clay reincarnated as the revolutonary confronting problems inherited from his contact with white culture. He returns to the home of his ex-wife, a white woman, and her husband, a literary critic. The play is essentially about Walker's attempt to destroy his white past. For it is the past, with all of its painful memories, that is really the enemy of the revolutionary. It is impossible to move until history is either re-created or comprehended. Unlike Todd, in Ralph Ellison's *Invisible Man,* Walker cannot fall outside history. Instead, Walker demands a confrontation with history, a final shattering of bullshit illusions. His only salvation lies in confronting the physical and psychological forces that have made him and his people powerless. Therefore, he comes to understand that the world must be restructured along spiritual imperatives. But in the interim it is basically a question of *who* has power:

EASLEY: You're so wrong about everything. So terribly, sickeningly wrong. What can you change? What do you hope to change? Do you think Negroes are better people than whites . . . that they can govern a society *better* than whites? That they'll be more judicious or more tolerant? Do you think they'll make fewer mistakes? I mean really, if the Western white man has proved one thing . . . it's the futility of modern society. So the have-not peoples become the haves. Even so, will that change the essential functions of the world? Will there be more love or beauty in the world . . . more knowledge . . . because of it?

WALKER: Probably Probably there will be more . . . if more people have a chance to understand what it is. But that's not even the point. It comes down to baser human endeavor than any social-political thinking. What does it matter if there's more love or beauty? Who the fuck cares? Is that what the Western ofay thought while he was ruling . . . that his rule somehow brought more love and beauty into the world? Oh, he might have thought that concomitantly, while sipping a gin rickey and scratching his ass . . . but that was not ever the point. Not even on the Crusades. The point is that you had your chance, darling, now these older folks have theirs. *Quietly*. Now they have theirs.

EASLEY: God, what an ugly idea.

This confrontation between the black radical and the white liberal is symbolic of larger confrontations occurring between the Third World and Western society. It is a confrontation between the colonizer and the colonized, the slave master and the slave. Implicit in Easley's remarks is the belief that the white man is culturally and politically superior to the black man. Even though Western society has been traditionally violent in its relation with the Third World, it sanctimoniously deplores violence or self-assertion on the part of the enslaved. And the Western mind, with clever rationalizations, equates the violence of the oppressed with the violence of the oppressor. So that when the native preaches self-determination, the Western white man cleverly misconstrues it to mean hate of *all* white men. When the black political radical warns his people not to trust white politicians of the Left and the Right, but instead to organize separately on the basis of power, the white man cries: "Racism in reverse." Or he will say, as many of them do today: "We deplore both white and black racism." As if the two could be equated.

There is a minor element in *The Slave* which assumes great importance in a later play entitled *Jello*. Here I refer to the emblem of Walker's army: a red-mouthed grinning field slave. The revolutionary army has taken one of the most hated symbols of the Afro-American past and radically altered its meaning.[1] This is the supreme act of freedom, available only to those who have liberated themselves psychically. Jones amplifies this inversion of emblem and symbol in *Jello* by making Rochester (Ratfester) of the old Jack Benny (Penny) program into a revolutionary nationalist. Ratfester, ordinarily the supreme embodiment of the Uncle Tom Clown, surprises Jack Penny by turning on the other side of the nature of the Black man. He skillfully, and with an evasive black humor, robs Penny of all of his money. But Ratfester's actions are "moral." That is to say, Ratfester is getting his back pay; payment of a long overdue debt to the Black man. Ratfester's sensibilities are different from Walker's. He is *blues people* smiling and shuffling while trying to figure out how to destroy the white thing. And like the blues man, he is the master of the understatement. Or in the Afro-American folk tradition, he is the Signifying Monkey, Shine, and Stackolee all rolled into one. There are no stereotypes anymore. History has killed Uncle Tom. Because even Uncle Tom has a breaking point beyond which he will not be pushed. Cut deeply enough into the most docile Negro, and you will find a conscious murderer. Behind the lyrics of the blues and the shuffling porter loom visions of white throats being cut and cities burning.

Jones's particular power as a playwright does not rest solely on his revolutionary vision, but is instead derived from his

deep lyricism and spiritual outlook. In many ways, he is fundamentally more a poet than a playwright. And it is his lyricism
that gives body to his plays. Two important plays in this regard
are *Black Mass* and *Slave Ship*. *Black Mass* is based on the
Muslim myth of Yacub. According to this myth, Yacub, a Black
scientist, developed the means of grafting different colors of
the Original Black Nation until a White Devil was created. In
Black Mass, Yacub's experiments produce a raving White Beast
who is condemned to the coldest regions of the North. The
other magicians implore Yacub to cease his experiments. But
he insists on claiming the primacy of scientific knowledge over
spiritual knowledge. The sensibility of the White Devil is alien,
informed by lust and sensuality. The Beast is the consummate
embodiment of evil, the beginning of the historical subjugation
of the spiritual world.

Black Mass takes place in some pre-historical time. In fact,
the concept of time, we learn, is the creation of an alien
sensibility, that of the Beast. This is a deeply weighted play, a
colloquy on the nature of man, and the relationship between
legitimate spritual knowledge and scientific knowledge. It is
LeRoi Jones's most important play mainly because it is informed by a mythology that is wholly the creation of the
Afro-American sensibility.

Further, Yacub's creation is not merely a scientific exercise.
More fundamentally, it is the aesthetic impulse gone astray.
The Beast is created merely for the sake of creation. Some
artists assert a similar claim about the nature of art. They argue
that art need not have a function. It is against this decadent
attitude toward art—rammed throughout most of Western
society—that they play militates. Yacub's real crime, therefore, is the introduction of a meaningless evil into a harmonious
universe. The evil of the Beast is pervasive, corrupting everything and everyone it touches. What was beautiful is twisted
into an ugly screaming thing. The play ends with the destruction
of the holy place of the Black Magicians. Now the Beast and his
descendants roam the earth. An off-stage voice chants a call for
the Jihad to begin. It is then that myth merges into legitimate
history, and we, the audience, come to understand that all
history is merely someone's version of mythology.

Slave Ship presents a more immediate confrontation with

history. In a series of expressionistic tableaux it depicts the horrors and the madness of the Middle Passage. It then moves through the period of slavery, early attempts at revolt, tendencies toward Uncle Tom-like reconciliation and betrayal, and the final act of liberation. There is no definite plot (LeRoi calls it a pageant), just a continuous rush of sound, moans, screams, and souls wailing for freedom and relief from suffering. This work has special attributes with the New Music of Sun Ra, John Coltrane, Albert Ayler, and Ornette Coleman. Events are blurred, rising and falling in a stream of sound. Almost cinematically, the images flicker and fade against a heavy backdrop of rhythm. The language is spare, stripped to the essential. It is a play which almost totally eliminates the need for a text. It functions on the basis of movement and energy, the dramatic equivalent of the New Music.

3.

LeRoi Jones is the best known and the most advanced playwright of the movement, but he is not alone. There are other excellent playwrights who express the general mood of the Black Arts ideology. Among them are Ron Milner, Ed Bullins, Ben Caldwell, Jimmy Stewart, Joe White, Charles Patterson, Charles Fuller, Aisha Hughes, Carol Freeman, and Jimmy Garrett.

Ron Milner's *Who's Got His Own* is of particular importance. It strips bare the clashing attitudes of a contemporary Afro-American family. Milner's concern is with legitimate manhood and morality. The family in *Who's Got His Own* is in search of its conscience, or more precisely its own definition of life. On the day of his father's death, Tim and his family are forced to examine the inner fabric of their lives, the lies, self-deceits, and sense of powerlessness in a white world. The basic conflict, however, is internal. It is rooted in the historical search for black manhood. Tim's mother is representative of a generation of Christian black women who have implicitly understood the brooding violence lurking in their men. And with this understanding, they have interposed themselves between their men and the object of that violence—the white man. Thus unable to direct his violence against the oppressor, the black man becomes more frustrated and the sense of powerlessness deepens. Lacking the strength to be a man in the white world, he turns against his family. So the oppressed, as Fanon explains, constantly dreams violence against his oppressor, while killing his brother on fast weekends.

Tim's sister represents the Negro woman's attempt to acquire what Eldridge Cleaver calls "ultrafemininity." That is, the attributes of her white upper-class counterpart. Involved here is a rejection of the body-oriented life of the working-class black man, symbolized by the mother's traditional religion. The sister has an affair with a white upper-class liberal, ending in abortion. There are hints of lesbianism, i.e., a further rejection of the body. The sister's life is a pivotal factor in the play. Much of the stripping away of falsehood initiated by Tim is directed at her life, which they have carefully kept hidden from the mother.

Tim is the product of the new Afro American sensibility, informed by the psychological revolution now operative within Black America. He is a combination ghetto soul-brother and militant intellectual, very hip and slightly flawed himself. He would change the world, but without comprehending the particular history that produced his "tyrannical" father. And he cannot be the man his father was—not until he truly understands his father. He must understand why his father allowed himself to be insulted daily by the "honky" types on the job; why he took a demeaning job in the "shit-house"; and why he spent on his family the violence that he should have directed against the white man. In short, Tim must confront the history of his family. And that is exactly what happens. Each character tells his story, exposing his falsehood to the other until a balance is reached.

Who's Got His Own is not the work of an alienated mind. Milner's main thrust is directed toward unifying the family around basic moral principles, toward bridging the "generation gap." Other black playwrights, Jimmy Garrett for example, see the gap as unbridgeable.

Garrett's We Own the Night takes place during an armed insurrection. As the play opens we see the central characters defending a section of the city against attacks by white police. Johnny, the protagonist, is wounded. Some of his Brothers intermittently fire at attacking forces, while others look for medical help. A doctor arrives, forced at gunpoint. The wounded boy's mother also comes. She is a female Uncle Tom who berates the Brothers and their cause. She tries to get Johnny to leave. She is hysterical. The whole idea of black people fighting white people is totally outside of her orientation. Johnny begins a vicious attack on his mother, accusing her of emasculating his father—a recurring theme in the sociology of the black community. In Afro-American literature of previous decades the strong black mother was the object of awe and respect. But in the new literature her status is ambivalent and laced with tension. Historically, Afro-American women have had to be the economic mainstays of the family. The oppressor allowed them to have jobs while at the same time limiting the economic mobility of the black man. Very often, therefore, the woman's aspirations and values are closely tied to those of the white power structure and not to those of her man. Since he cannot provide for his family the way white men do, she despises his weakness, tearing into him at every opportunity until, very often, there is nothing left but a shell.

The only way out of this dilemma is through revolution. It either must be an actual blood revolution, or one that psychically redirects the energy of the oppressed. Milner is fundamentally concerned with the latter, and Garrett with the former. Communication between Johnny and his mother breaks down. The revolutionary imperative demands that men step outside the legal framework. It is a question of erecting *another* morality. The old constructs do not hold up because adhering to them means consigning oneself to the oppressive reality. Johnny's mother is involved in the old constructs. Manliness is equated with white morality. And even though she claims to love her family (her men), the overall design of her ideas are against black manhood. In Garrett's play the mother's morality manifests itself in a deep-seated hatred of black men, while in Milner's work the mother understands, but holds her men back.

The mothers that Garrett and Milner see represent the Old Spirituality—the Faith of the Fathers of which DuBois spoke. Johnny and Tim represent the New Spirituality. They appear to be a type produced by the upheavals of the colonial world of which black America is a part. Johnny's assertion that he is a criminal is remarkably similar to the rebel's comments in Aimé Césaire's play *Les Armes Miraculeuses (The Miraculous Weapons)*. In that play the rebel, speaking to his mother, proclaims: "My name—an offense; my Christian name—humiliation; my status—a rebel; my age—the stone age." To which the mother replies: "My race—the human race. My religion—brotherhood." The Old Spirituality is generalized. It seeks to recognize Universal Humanity. The New Spirituality is specific. It begins by seeing the world from the concise point of view of the colonialized. Where the Old Spirituality would live with oppression while ascribing to the oppressors an innate goodness, the New Spirituality demands a radical shift in point of view. The colonialized native, the oppressed must, of necessity, subscribe to a *separate* morality. One that will liberate him and his people.

The assault against the Old Spirituality can sometimes be humorous. In Ben Caldwell's play *The Militant Preacher* a burglar is seen slipping into the home of a wealthy minister. The preacher comes in and the burglar ducks behind a large chair. The preacher, acting out the role of the supplicant minister, begins to moan, praying to De Lawd for understanding.

In the context of today's politics, the minister is an Uncle Tom, mouthing platitudes against self-defense. The preacher drones in a self-pitying monologue about the folly of protecting oneself against brutal policemen. Then the burglar begins to speak. The preacher is startled, taking the burglar's voice for the voice of God. The burglar begins to play on the preacher's old-time religion. He *becomes* the voice of God insulting and goading the preacher on until the preacher's attitudes about protective violence change. The next day the preacher emerges militant, gun in hand, wounding like Reverend [Albert Buford] Cleage in Detroit. He now preaches a new gospel—the gospel of the gun, an eye for an eye. The gospel is preached in the rhythmic cadences of the old black church. But the content is radical. Just as Jones inverted the symbols in *Jello*, Caldwell twists the rhythms of the Uncle Tom preacher into the language of the new militancy.

These plays are directed at problems within black America. They begin with the premise that there is a well-defined Afro-

American audience. An audience that must see itself and the world in terms of its own interests. These plays, along with many others, constitute the basis for a viable movement in the theater—a movement which takes as its task a profound reevaluation of the black man's presence in America. The Black Arts Movement represents the flowering of a cultural nationalism that has been suppressed since the 1920s. I mean the "Harlem Renaissance"—which was essentially a failure. It did not address itself to the mythology and the life-styles of the black community. It failed to take root, to link itself concretely to the struggles of that community, to become its voice and spirit. Implicit in the Black Arts Movement is the idea that black people, however dispersed, constitute a *nation* within the belly of white America. This is not a new idea. Garvey said it and the Honorable Elijah Muhammad says it now. And it is on this idea that the concept of Black Power is predicated.

Afro-American life and history is full of creative possibilities, and the movement is just beginning to perceive them. Just beginning to understand that the most meaningful statements about the nature of Western society must come from the Third World of which black America is a part. The thematic material is broad, ranging from folk heroes like Shine and Stackolee to historical figures like Marcus Garvey and Malcolm X. And then there is the struggle for black survival, the coming confrontation between white America and black America. If art is the harbinger of future possibilities, what does it portend for the future of black America?

1968

NOTE

1. In Jones's study of Afro-American music, *Blues People,* we find the following observation: "Even the adjective *funky,* which once meant to many Negroes merely a stink (usually associated with sex), was used to qualify the music as meaningful (the word became fashionable and is now almost useless). The social implication, then, was that even the old stereotype of a distinctive Negro smell that white America subscribed to could be turned against white America. For this smell now, real or not, was made a valuable characteristic of 'Negro-ness.' And 'Negro-ness,' by the fifties, for many Negroes (and whites) was the only strength left to American culture."

The Genuis and the Prize

"Fate's being kind to me. . . . Fate doesn't want me to be too famous too young."

These were the words of Duke Ellington when he learned that the Pulitzer Prize advisory board had turned down the music jury's citation of Ellington for his achievements in modern music over a long period. The jury had in mind the sum total of Duke Ellington's work. We will return to this point.

The question is: How should we feel about this? Should we rather feel the Duke was cheated out of a well-deserved award; cheated out of recognition by the creative establishment—that's what the Pulitzer is—which has been long overdue? The manner in which this question is answered is ultimately related to how we see ourselves vis-à-vis the dominant society—white America. Should we really be concerned about recognition from a society that oppresses us, exploits us; and which will even use its "acceptance" of us as another instrument of enslavement? This time the enslavement is more psychological than physical.

This kind of enslavement furthers the idea of a liberal America, abundantly aware of the creative gifts of the black man; it further reinforces our dependency upon white America.

All of this is not to say that Duke or anybody else receiving these awards should refuse them. (That wouldn't be a bad idea, though.) I am proposing that what we understand is the necessity of establishing our own norms, our own values; and if there must be standards, let them be our own. Recognition of Duke Ellington's genius lies not with the white society that has exploited him and his fellow musicians. It lies with us, the black public, black musicians and artists. Essentially, recognition of that sort, from a society that hates us and has no real way of evaluating our artistic accomplishments, is the meanest kind of intrusion upon the territory of black people.

We dig you, Duke. We play your music, sing your songs, and feel their relationship to our everyday life and needs. These are the words that must flow out of an organized body of black musicians or some black institutions. They are the words of brothers, and they act to reaffirm group consciousness and group obligation. They act to establish, once and for all, that we are collectively aware of our own artistic talents and that recognition from white America is simply incidental to recognition from black America.

Recognition from dominant white society should not be the primary aim of the black artist. He must decide that his art belongs primarily to his own people. This is not to deny that there are some "universal" factors at work; but we are living in a specific place, at a specific time, and are a specific set of people with a specific historical development. In the confusion of today's struggle for human survival, the black artist can not afford vagueness about himself and his people who need him.

Duke's approach to music has always been rooted in the materials found naturally among black people. His work stands as a monumental achievement in precision and form. Duke has never ceased to be an innovator. And we must feel that the sum total of his work belongs to us; it is we who must say what it is; it is we who must give the awards.[1]

NOTE

1. Acting Mayor Paul Screvane later gave Ellington a citation on behalf of the city of New York.

Eatonville's Zora Neale Hurston: A Profile

Among the literary figures that emerged from the all-too brief black cultural upsurgence of the Harlem Renaissance, Zora Neale Hurston was one of the most significant and, ironically, one of the least well known. She was one of the first black writers to attempt a serious study of black folklore and folk history and as such was a precursor of the interest in folkways that shapes much of contemporary black fiction. Her comparative present-day anonymity, then, is surprising, but is perhaps explained by the complexity of her personality and the controversy that attended her career.

Writing in the May 1928 edition of the *The World Tomorrow*, Zora Neale Hurston made the following observation about herself: "Sometimes, I feel discriminated against, but it does not make me angry. It merely astonishes me. How can anyone deny themselves the pleasure of my company!" This is the kind of remark that one came to expect from Miss Hurston, who is remembered as one of the most publicly flamboyant personalities of the Harlem literary movement. She was very bold and outspoken, an attractive woman who had learned how to survive with native wit. She approached life as a series of encounters and challenges; most of these she overcame without succumbing to the maudlin bitterness of many of her contemporaries.

In her autobiography, *Dust Tracks on a Road*, she explains her life as a series of migrations, of wanderings, the first of these beginning with the death of her mother. She then went to live with relatives who very often could not relate to her fantasy-oriented approach to life. As a child, she nearly lived inside of books. She may have been something of a show-off, and this would have probably annoyed her relatives, who were hardworking people and therefore concerned with the more fundamental aspects of life. Consequently, she was shuttled back and forth among relatives who found her a somewhat difficult child to rear.

She was totally dependent upon them for survival, but she refused to humble herself to them:

> A child in my place ought to realize I was lucky to have a roof over my head and anything to eat at all. And from their point of view, they were right. From mine, my stomach pains were the least of my sufferings. I wanted what they could not conceive of. I could not reveal myself for lack of expression, and then for lack of hope of understanding, even if I could have found the words. I was not comfortable to have around. Strange things must have looked out of my eyes like Lazarus after his resurrection.

She was fourteen years old when she began taking jobs as a maid. Several of these jobs ended in disappointment. She was in a difficult position. She was a Southern black child who was forced by economic necessity to make a living. But if given a choice between performing her duties as a maid or reading a book from the library of an employer, she almost always chose reading the book. She describes this period of her life as "restless" and "unstable."

But she was finally fortunate enough to acquire a position as maid to an actress. This position represented a significant break with the parochialism of her rural background and opened the way for her entry into creative activity as a way of life. Here, at last, she could exploit her fantasies. Here she could be the entertainer and the entertained. And most importantly, for this small-town Southerner, she could travel and seriously begin to bring some shape to her vagabond existence.

Black people have almost boundless faith in the efficacy of education. Traditionally, it has represented the chief means of overcoming the adversities of slavery; it is the group's main index of concrete achievement. Zora shared that attitude toward education. It is a central motif throughout her autobiography. Education, for her, became something of a Grail-like quest. As soon as she was situated in a school she would have to leave in order to seek employment, usually as a maid or a babysitter. But her life experiences and her reading were an education in themselves. By the time she entered Morgan College in Baltimore, she was sophisticated, in a homey sort of way, and tough. She had personality and an open manner that had the effect of disarming all of those who came in touch with her. But none of this would have meant anything if she had been without talent.

After a short stay at Morgan College, she was given a recommendation to Howard University in Washington, D.C. There she soon came under the influence of Lorenzo Dow Turner, who was head of the English department. He was a significant influence. Like Leo Hansberry (also of Howard), Turner is one of those unsung heroes of Afro-American scholarship. He is the author of an important monograph on African linguistic features in Afro-American speech. It was while Zora was at Howard that she also published her first short story, "Drenched in Light" in *Opportunity*, a magazine edited by Charles S. Johnson. Her second short story, also published in *Opportunity*, won her an award, a secretarial job with Fannie Hurst, and a scholarship to Barnard. There, she came under the influence of Franz Boas, the renowned anthropologist. It was Boas who suggested that she seriously undertake the study of African-American folklore—a pursuit that was to mold her contribution to black American literature.

Zora Neale Hurston was born in 1901 in the all-black town of Eatonville, Florida. This town and other places in Florida figure quite prominently in much of her work, especially her fiction. Her South was, however, vastly different from the South depicted in the works of Richard Wright. Wright's fictional landscape was essentially concerned with the psychological ramifications of racial oppression, and black people's response to it. Zora, on the other hand, held a different point of view. For her, in spite of its hardships, the South was Home. It was not a place from which one escaped, but rather, the place to which one returned for spiritual revitalization. It was a place where one remembered with fondness and nostalgia the taste of soulfully prepared cuisine. Here one recalled the poetic eloquence of the local preacher (Zora's father had been one himself). For her also, the South represented a place with a distinct cultural tradition. Here one heard the best church choirs in the world, and experienced the great expanse of green fields.

When it came to the South, Zora could often be an inveterate romantic. In her work, there are no bellboys shaking in fear before brutal tobacco-chewing crackers. Neither are there any black men being pursued by lynch mobs. She was not concerned with these aspects of the Southern reality. We could accuse her of escapism, but the historical oppression that we now associate with Southern black life was not a central aspect of her experience.

Perhaps it was because she was a black woman, and therefore not considered a threat to anyone's system of social values. One thing is clear, though: Unlike Richard Wright, she was no political radical. She was, instead, a belligerent individualist who was decidedly unpredictable and perhaps a little inconsistent. At one moment she could sound highly nationalistic. Then at other times she might mouth statements that, in terms of the ongoing struggle for Black liberation, were ill conceived and even reactionary.

Needless to say, she was a very complex individual. Her acquaintances ranged from the blues people of the jooks and the turpentine camps in the South to the upper-class literati of New York City. She had been Fannie Hurst's secretary, and Carl Van Vechten had been a friend throughout most of her professional career. These friendships were, for the most part, genuine, even if they do smack somewhat of opportunism on Zora's part. For it was the Van Vechten and Nancy Cunard types who exerted a tremendous amount of power over the Harlem literary movement. For this element, and others, Zora appears to have been something of a cultural showcase. They clearly enjoyed her company, and often "repaid" her by bestowing all kinds of favors upon her.

In this connection, one of the most interesting descriptions of her is found in Langston Hughes's autobiography, *The Big Sea:*

In her youth, she was always getting scholarships
and things from wealthy white people, some of whom
simply paid her just to sit around and represent the
Negro race for them, she did it in such a racy fashion. She was full of sidesplitting anecdotes, humorous tales, and tragicomic stories, remembered out of
her life in the South as the daughter of a traveling
minister of God. She could make you laugh one
moment and cry the next. To many of her white
friends, no doubt, she was a perfect "darkie," in the
nice meaning they give the term—that is a naive,
childlike, sweet humorous, and highly colored Negro.

According to Mr. Hughes, she was also an intelligent person,
who was clever enough never to allow her college education to
alienate her from the folk culture that became the central
impulse in her life's work.

It was in the field of folklore that she did probably her most
commendable work. With the possible exception of Sterling
Brown, she was the only important writer of the Harlem literary movement to undertake a systematic study of African-
American folklore. The movement had as one of its stated goals
the reevaluation of African-American history and folk culture.
But there appears to have been very little work done in these
areas by the Harlem literati. There was, however, a general
awareness of the literary possibilities of Black folk culture—
witness the blues poetry of Langston Hughes and Sterling
Brown. But generally speaking, very few writers of the period
committed themselves to intensive research and collection of
folk materials. This is especially ironic given the particular
race consciousness of the twenties and thirties.

Therefore, vital areas of folkloristic scholarship went unex-
plored. What this means, in retrospect, is that the development
of a truly original literature would be delayed until black
writers came to grips with the cultural ramifications of the
African presence in America. Because black literature would
have to be, in essence, the most profound, the most intensely
human expression of the ethos of a people, this literature would
realize its limitless possibilities only after creative writers had
come to some kind of understanding of the specific, as well as
general, ingredients that must enter into the shaping of an

African culture in America. In order to do this, it would be necessary to establish some new categories of perception; new ways of seeing a culture that had been caricatured by the white minstrel tradition, made hokey and sentimental by the nineteenth-century local colorists, debased by the dialect poets, and finally made a "primitive" aphrodisiac by the new sexualism of the twenties.

And to further complicate matters, the writer would have to grapple with the full range of literary technique and innovation that the English language had produced. Content and integrity of feeling aside, much of the writing of the so-called Harlem Renaissance is a pale reflection of outmoded conventional literary technique. Therefore, the Harlem literary movement failed in two essential categories, that of form and that of sensibility. Form relates to the manner in which literary technique is executed, while sensibility, as used here, pertains to the cluster of psychological, emotional, and psychic states that have their basis in mythology and folklore. In other words, we are talking about the projection of an ethos through literature; that is, the projection of the characteristic sensibility of a nation, or of a specific sociocultural group.

In terms of the consummate uses of the folk sensibility, the Harlem movement leaves much to be desired. There was really no encounter and subsequent grappling with the visceral elements of the Black experience but rather a tendency on the part of many of the movement's writers to pander to the voguish concerns of the white social circles in which they found themselves.

But Zora's interest in folklore gave her a slight edge on some of her contemporaries. Her first novel, *Jonah's Gourd Vine* (1934), is dominated by a gospellike feeling, but it is somewhat marred by its awkward use of folk dialect. In spite of this problem, she manages to capture, to a great extent, the inner reality of a religious man who is incapable of resisting the enticements of the world of flesh. She had always maintained that the black preacher was essentially a poet, in fact, the only true poet to which the race could lay claim. In a letter to James Weldon Johnson, April 16, 1934, speaking of *Jonah's Gourd Vine,* she wrote:

I have tried to present a Negro preacher who is neither funny nor an imitation Puritan ram-rod in pants. Just the human being and poet that he must be to succeed in a Negro pulpit. I do not speak of those among us who have been tampered with and consequently have gone Presbyterian or Episcopal. I mean the common run of us who love magnificence, beauty, poetry and color so much so that there can never be too much of it.

The poetic aspect of the black sermon was one of her central concerns at the time of the publication of *Jonah's Gourd Vine;* by then she had begun systematically to study and collect Afro-American folklore and was especially interested in isolating those features that indicated a unique sensibility was at work in African-American folk expression. In this connection, she wrote an essay for Nancy Cunard's anthology *Negro* (1934) entitled "Characteristics of Negro Expression." A rather lightweight piece really. But it is important because it does illustrate one central characteristic of African-derived cultures. And that is the principle of "acting things out." She writes: "Every phase of Negro life is highly dramatized. No matter how joyful or how sad the case there is sufficient poise for drama. Everything is acted out." She saw the black preacher as the principal dramatic figure in the socioreligious lives of black people.

Commenting to James Weldon Johnson on a *New York Times* review of *Jonah's Gourd Vine*, she complains that the reviewer failed to understand how the preacher in her novel "could have so much poetry in him." In this letter of May 8, 1934, she writes:

> When you and I (who seem to be the only ones even among Negroes who recognize the barbaric poetry in their sermons) know there are hundreds of preachers who are equalling that sermon, the one in *Jonah's Gourd Vine* weekly. He does not know that merely being a good man is not enough to hold a Negro preacher in an important charge. He must also be an artist. He must be both a poet and an actor of a very high order, and then he must have the voice and figure.

Her second novel, *Their Eyes Were Watching God* (1937), is clearly her best novel. This work indicates that she had a rather remarkable understanding of a blues aesthetic and its accompanying sensibility. Paraphrasing Ellison's definition of the blues: This novel confronts the most intimate and brutal aspects of personal catastrophe and renders them lyrically. She is inside of a distinct emotional environment here. This is a passionate, somewhat ironic love story—perhaps a little too rushed in parts—but written with a great deal of sensitivity to character and locale.

It was written in Haiti "under internal pressure in seven weeks," and represents a concentrated release of emotional energy that is rather carefully shaped and modulated by Zora's compassionate understanding of Southern black life-styles. Here she gathers together several themes that were used in previous work: the nature of love, the search for personal freedom, the clash between spiritual and material aspirations, and, finally, the quest for a more than parochial range of life experiences.

The novel has a rather simple framework: Janie, a black woman of great beauty, returns to her hometown and is immediately the subject of vaguely malicious gossip concerning her past and her lover Tea Cake. Janie's only real friend in the town is an elderly woman called Pheoby. It is to her that Janie tells her deeply poignant story. Under pressure from a strict grandmother, Janie is forced into an unwanted marriage. Her husband is not necessarily a rich man; however, he is resourceful and hardworking. In his particular way, he represents the more oppressive aspects of the rural life. For him, she is essentially a workhorse.

After taking as much as she can, she cuts out with Joe Starks, whose style and demeanor seem to promise freedom from her oppressive situation. She describes him:

> It was a citified, stylish dressed man with his hat set at an angle that didn't belong in these parts. His coat was over his arm, but he didn't need it to represent his clothes. The shirt with the silk sleeveholders was dazzling enough for the world. He whistled, mopped his face and walked like he knew where he was going. He was a seal-brown color but he acted like

Mr. Washburn or somebody like that to Janie. Where
would such a man be coming from and where was he
going? He didn't look her way nor no other way
except straight ahead, so Janie ran to the pump and
jerked the handle hard while she pumped. It made a
loud noise and also made her heavy hair fall down.
So he stopped and looked hard, and then he asked
her for a cool drink of water. (See Zora's short story
"The Gilded Six-bits" for another example of the
clash between the urban and rural sensibility in
Langston Hughes's *The Best Short Stories by Negro
Writers* [Boston: Little, Brown & Co., 1967].)

She later leaves her husband, and takes up with Joe Starks,
who is clearly a man with big ideas. He has a little money,
people love him, and he is an excellent organizer. But Janie
does not really occupy a central emotional concern in Joe's
scheme of things. She is merely a reluctant surrogate in his
quest for small-town power and prestige. Joe is envied by
everyone for having so much organizational and economic ability. But his lovely wife, who represents an essential aspect of
his personal achievements, is basically frustrated and unloved.
After several years, Joe Starks dies. The marriage itself had
died years ago. She had conformed to Joe's idea of what a
woman of influence and prestige should be. But again, she had
not been allowed to flower, to experience life on her own
terms.

The last third of the novel concerns Janie's life with Tea
Cake, a gambler and itinerant worker. Tea Cake represents the
dynamic, unstructured energy of the folk. He introduces her to
a wider range of emotional experience. He is rootless, tied to
no property save that which he carries with him, and he is not
adverse to gambling that away if the opportunity presents
itself. But he is warm and sensitive. He teaches her whatever
she wants to know about his life and treats her with a great
deal of respect. In spite of the implicit hardship of their lives,
she has never lived life so fully and with such an expanse of
feeling. And here is where Zora introduces her characteristic
irony.

While working in the Everglades, they are nearly destroyed
by a mean tropical storm. They decide to move to high ground

and are forced to make their way across a swollen river. (The storm is described in vivid details that bear interesting allusions to Bessie Smith's "Backwater Blues.") A mad dog threatens Janie, and while protecting her Tea Cake is bitten. He contracts rabies, and later is himself so maddened by the infection that he begins to develop dangerous symptoms of paranoia. He threatens to kill Janie, and in self-defense she is forced to kill him. This is the story that she tells Pheoby.

But there is no hint of self-pity here. Just an awesome sense of the utter inability of man to fully order his life comparatively free of outside forces. Zora Neale Hurston was not an especially philosophical person, but she was greatly influenced by the religious outlook of the black church. So that this novel seems often informed by a subtle, though persistent, kind of determinism. She has a way of allowing catastrophe to descend upon her characters at precisely the moment when they have achieved some insight into the fundamental nature of their lives. She introduces disruptive forces into essentially harmonious situations. And the moral fiber of her characters is always tested. Usually, in a contest between the world of flesh and the world of spirit, she has her characters succumb to the flesh.

However, she has no fixed opinions about relationships between men and women. She can bear down bitterly on both of them. She will allow a good woman to succumb to temptation just as quickly as a man. And when such things occur with couples who genuinely love each other, she has a way of illustrating the spiritual redemption that is evident even in moral failure. She is clearly a student of male/female relationships. And when she is not being too "folksy," she has the ability to penetrate to the core of the emotional context in which her characters find themselves. In this regard, she was in advance of many of her "renaissance" contemporaries. There are very few novels of the period written with such compassion and love for black people.

In *Moses, Man of the Mountain* (1939), she retells the story of the Biblical Moses. Naturally, she attempts to overlay it with a black idiom. She makes Moses a hoodoo man with African-derived magical powers. She is apparently attempting to illustrate a possible parallel between the ancient Hebrew search for a nation and the struggles of black people in America, and she is moderately successful.

The Bible had always been of special importance to her. It was the first book that she read seriously. Her father was a preacher. Further, the Bible is the most prominent piece of literature in the homes of most black families, especially in the South. The title of her first novel comes from the Bible. In a letter to Carl Van Vechten, she explains: "You see the Prophet of God sat up under a gourd vine that had grown up in one night. But a cut-worm came along and cut it down. . . . One act of malice and it is withered and gone. The book of a thousand million leaves was closed." And finally, in further correspondence to Carl Van Vechten, she expresses a desire to write another novel on the Jews. This one was to be of immense scope. It was to be based on the premise that Moses and the Levites were actually oppressors of the Jews, and not necessarily their liberators. She notes, for example, that these "oppressors" forbade the writing of other books. So that in three thousand years, she points out, only twenty-two books of the Bible were written. The novel was never published, but its working title was "Under Fire and Cloud."

Her last novel is a sometimes turgid romance entitled *Seraph on the Suwanee* (1948). Its central characters are white Southerners. It is competently written, but commands no compelling significance. Since she was often in need of money, she may have intended it as a better-than-average potboiler.

She made her most significant contribution to black literature in the field of folkloristic research. *Mules and Men* (1935) is a collection of African-American folktales; it also gives a rather vivid account of the practice of hoodoo in Louisiana. *Tell My Horse* (1938), a book about Jamaican and Haitian culture, is perhaps one of the important accounts of voodoo rites and practices in print anywhere. It successfully competes with most of the books on the subject, and there are quite a few of them. An interesting aspect of both of these books, especially *Tell My Horse*, is the complete manner in which she insinuates herself into whatever kind of sociocultural event she is trying to understand.

Both in Louisiana and Haiti, she allowed herself to be initiated into the various rites to which she had devoted her studies. Therefore, in order to learn the internal workings of these rites, she repeatedly submitted herself to the rigorous demands of the "two-headed" hoodoo doctors of New Orleans and the voodoo hougans of Haiti. She was an excellent observer of the folkloristic and ritualistic process. Further, she approached her subject with the engaged sensibility of the artist; she left the "comprehensive" scientific approach to culture to men like her former teacher Franz Boas, and to Melville Herskovits. Her approach to folklore research was essentially freewheeling and activist in style. She would have been very uncomfortable as a scholar committed to "pure research."

She had learned from experience that the folk collector must in some manner identify with her subject. For her the collector should be a willing participant in the myth-ritual process. Her actions in some of this research seem to indicate that she had nothing against assuming a persona whenever it was necessary. Given the dramatic nature of her personality, it was highly possible; we can be almost certain that she carried off her transformation into ritual participant exceptionally well. Such was not the case when she first began her research while still a student at Barnard College:

> My first six months (collecting folk materials) were disappointing. I found out later that it was not because I had no talent for research, but because I did not have the right approach. The glamour of Barnard College was still upon me. I dwelt in Marble Halls. I knew where the material was, all right. But I went about asking, in carefully accented Barnardese, "Pardon me, but do you know any folk-tales or folk-songs?" The men and women who had whole treasuries of material just seeping through their pores looked at me and shook their heads. No, they had never heard of anything like that around there. Maybe it was over in the next county. Why didn't I try over there? I did, and got the self-same answer.

This disappointed her for a while. But soon she discovered exactly how her own background in the South had so thoroughly imbued her with the natural attributes of a good folklore researcher. She remembered that her own Eatonville was rich in oral materials. In a sense, you could say that she realized that she, Zora Neale Hurston, was finally folk herself, in spite of the Guggenheim Fellowship and the degree from Barnard College. Here she is, in *Mules and Men*, blending into her materials:

> "Ah come to collect some old stories and tales and Ah know y'all know a plenty of 'em and that's why Ah headed straight for home."
>
> "What you mean, Zora, them old lies we tell when we're jus' sittin' around here on the store porch doin' nothin'?" asked B. Mosely.
>
> "Yeah those same ones about Ole Massa and colored folks in heaven, and—oh y'all know the kind I mean."

Zora had a way of implicitly assuming that the world view of her subjects was relatively accurate and justified on its own terms. For example, she rarely, if ever, questioned the integrity or abilities of a hougan, or hoodoo doctor. Likewise, she never denigrates her subjects or their rituals, which to the Western mind may smack of savagery. What she sees and experiences, therefore, is what you get. This is particularly true of those cases in which we find her both the narrator and the participant in a ritual experience. Here is another selection from *Mules and Men*:

> I entered the old pink stucco house in Vieux Carré at nine o'clock in the morning with the parcel of needed things. Turner placed the new underwear on the big Altar; prepared the couch with the snake-skin cover upon which I was to lie for three days. With the help of other members of the college of hoodoo doctors called together to initiate me, the snake skins I had brought were made into garments for me to wear. One was coiled into a high headpiece—the crown. One had loops attached to slip on my arms so that it could be worn as a shawl, and the other was made into a girdle for my loins. All places have significance. These garments were placed on the small altar in the corner. The throne of the snake. The Great One was called upon to enter the garments and dwell there.
>
> I was made ready and at three o'clock in the

afternoon, naked as I came into the world, I was
stretched, face downwards, my navel to the snakeskin cover, and began my three-day search for the
spirit that he might accept or reject me according to
his will. Three days my body must lie silent and
fasting while my spirit went wherever spirits must go
that seek answers never given to men as men.

I could have no food, but a pitcher of water was
placed on a small table at the head of the couch, that
my spirit might not waste time in search of water
which should be spent in search of the Power-Giver.
The spirit must have water, and if none had been
provided it would wander in search of it. And evil
spirits might attack it as it wandered about dangerous places. If it should be seriously injured, it might
never return to me.

For sixty-nine hours I lay there. I had five psychic
experiences and awoke at last with no feeling of
hunger, only one of exaltation.

Her autobiography, *Dust Tracks on a Road*, helps to give us
a fundamental sense of the emotional tenor of her life. It was a
life full of restless energy and movement. It was a somewhat
controversial life in many respects, for she was not above
commerical popularization of black culture. And many of her
contemporaries considered her a pseudofolksy exhibitionist or,
worse, a Sol Hurok of black culture. One elderly Harlem
writer recalls that she once gave a party to which she invited
white and Negro friends. Zora is supposed to have worn a red
bandanna (Aunt Jemima style), while serving her guests something like collard greens and pigs' feet. The incident may be
apocryphal. Many incidents surrounding the lives of famous
people are. But the very existence of such tales acts to illustrate
something central to a person's character. Zora was a kind of
Pearl Bailey of the literary world. If you can dig the connection.

As we have already stated, she was no political radical. To
be more precise, she was something of a conservative in her
political outlook. For example, she unquestionably believed in
the efficacy of American democracy, even when that democracy came under very serious critical attack from the white and
black Left of the twenties and thirties. Her conservatism was

composed of a naive blend of honesty and boldness. She was not above voicing opinions that ran counter to the prevailing thrust of the civil rights movement. For example, she was against the Supreme Court decision of 1954. She felt that the decision implied a lack of competency on the part of black teachers, and hence she saw it as essentially an insult to black people.

After a fairly successful career as a writer, she suddenly dropped out of the creative scene after 1948. Why she did this is somewhat of a minor enigma. She was at the apex of her career. Her novel *Seraph on the Suwanee* had received rather favorable reviews, and her letters to Carl Van Vechten indicated that she had a whole host of creative ideas kicking around inside of her.

Perhaps the answer lies in an incident that happened in the fall of 1948. At that time she was indicted on a morals charge. The indictment charged that she had been a party in sexual relationships with two mentally ill boys and an older man. The charge was lodged by the mother of the boys. All of the evidence indicates that it was a false charge; Zora was out of the country at the time of the alleged crime. But several of the Negro newspapers exploded it into a major scandal. Naturally, Zora was hurt. And the incident plunged her into a state of abject despair. She was proud of America and extremely patriotic. She believed that even though there were some obvious faults in the American system of government, they were minimal, or at worst the aberrations of a few sick, unrepresentative individuals. This incident made her question the essential morality of the American legal system.

In a letter to her friend Carl Van Vechten she wrote:

> I care for nothing anymore. My country has failed me utterly. My race has seen fit to destroy me without reason, and with the vilest tools conceived of by man so far. A society, eminently Christian, and supposedly devoted to super decency has gone so far from its announced purpose, not to protect children, but to exploit the gruesome fancies of a pathological case and do this thing to human decency. Please do not forget that thing was not done in the South, but in the so-called liberal North. Where shall I look in

the country for justice. . . . All that I have tried to do has proved useless. All that I have believed in has failed me. I have resolved to die. It will take me a few days for me to set my affairs in order, then I will go.

There was no trial. The charges were dropped. And Zora Neale Hurston ceased to be a creative writer. In the early fifties, she wrote some articles for the *Saturday Evening Post* and the conservative *American Legion* magazine. She took a job as a maid; and after a story of hers appeared in the *Post*, her employers discovered her true background and told all of their friends. Stories later appeared in many newspapers around the country, telling of the successful Negro writer who was now doing housework. One story, in the *St. Louis Post-Dispatch*, quotes her as saying: "You can use your mind only so long. . . . Then you have to use your hands. It's just the natural thing. I was born with a skillet in my hands. Why shouldn't I do it for somebody else awhile? A writer has to stop writing every now and then and live a little. You know what I mean?" James Lyons, the reporter, goes on to say: "Miss Hurston believes she is temporarily 'written out.' An eighth novel and three short stories are now in the hands of her agents and she feels it would be sensible to 'shift gears' for a few months."

But none of her plans ever materialized. She died penniless on January 28, 1960, in the South she loved so much.

1972

Uncle Rufus Raps on the Squared Circle

Once I saw a prize fighter boxing a yokel. The fighter was swift and amazingly scientific. His body was one violent flow of rapid rhythmic action. He hit the yokel a hundred times while the yokel held up his arms in stunned surprise. But suddenly the yokel, rolling about in the gale of boxing gloves, struck one blow and knocked science, speed and footwork as cold as a well-digger's posterior. The smart money hit the canvas. The long shot got the nod. The yokel had simply stepped inside of his opponent's sense of time.

—Ralph Ellison, *Invisible Man*

Sporting events, like beauty contests, horse shows, public assassinations—all forms of spectacle—have implicit within them a distinct metaphysical character, said Uncle Rufus while lighting his cigar. We had been talking about the Ali-Frazier fight. He had once been a boxer. Then later he became a singer and dancer in a minstrel show. Needless to say, Uncle Rufus is a most fascinating gentleman. Following our discussion, I discovered that he was one of the prime sources for Melvin B. Tolson's extremely muscular masterpiece entitled, *"The Harlem Gallery."* Further, Uncle Rufus staunchly maintains that he knew the real John Henry who, by the way, was an excellent bare-knuckle fighter.

The day after the Ali-Frazier fight, I met him uptown at a little spot in Harlem called My Bar. The bar is a very hip joint.

It's run by a tall yellow guy named Julian May. It's a good place to talk all kinds of sports. Julian's got himself a brand-new color TV in the back room. And there's a bartender there, Ray, who is a statistical and historical expert on all sports, especially the ones in which we dominate, or the ones in which we have determined the stylistic mode and strategy. But Ray would never speak in these terms; he absorbs his data on sports because he loves them and sees them as significant encounters with the unknowable nature of the world. Ray's attitude toward sports like boxing, football and basketball is a healthy blend of the mysterious and scientific.

I am sitting at the bar, discussing with Ray the function of energy in athletics when Uncle Rufus bops into the door. He peacocks in a pearl gray homburg. The coat is blue cashmere. He sports a golden-headed serpent cane; the shoes, French, Shriner and Urner, contrast exquisitely with his spats which are the same pearl gray color as the homburg.

I order him a Jack Daniels, and introduce him to Ray. A discussion ensues concerning the geometry of basketball. I feel shut out of the conversation; and besides, I didn't invite my uncle here to talk about basketball. I was really getting irritated with the whole thing when some customers finally worked into the bar.

So now that I had Uncle Rufus to myself, I asked him his opinion of the Ali-Frazier fight. He began the discussion with some commentary on a few of the events that transpired in the aftermath of Jack Johnson's victory over Jim Jeffries back in Reno on July 4, 1910.

"It was during the days of the steamboat, and after that famous bout," he said, "there was fighting going on between the blacks and whites. This happened because the whites were so infuriated by Jack's victory that they began beating up on the colored. A man got lynched in Cap Giradeau when he tried to collect a bet he had made with a white farmer by the name of Cyrus Compton.

"I was working on a show called Stall's Minstrels. Now this show was out of Cairo, Illinois, which is smack on the Mississippi River. But we was working in a dance hall in Henderson, Kentucky. I think they called that hall The Stomp. All the great troupes had worked it. The Creole Show and Black Patti's

Troubadours had also been through there. And while I was in Henderson, I heard a splendid concert of operatic selections by Sissieretta Jones."

"Well, what about the fight?" I asked.

"Oh . . . the fight? Which fight?"

"It's hard to tell now; I asked you about the Ali-Frazier fight, and you started talking about Jack Johnson which, it seems to me, doesn't have much to do with this conversation."

"Let's put it this way son: You order me another one of these Jack Daniels, and sit back patiently so you can learn something for once in your life."

"If you wasn't my Uncle Rufus, I would tell you to go and eat shit, talking to me that way."

"Never mind that . . . I want it on the rocks with water on the side."

I ordered the drink. Ray came over, poured his drink, then mine. I think I saw them exchange winks.

"Well, as I was trying to say, I was in Henderson, and I heard that they was fighting and all."

"Who was fighting and all?"

"The colored and white."

"They say, no sooner did Jack win the match than the fighting broke out. Well, I was in Henderson, and I heard that they was fighting in Evansville, Indiana. Evansville is right across the Ohio River from Henderson, so I went up there. Man, even with the fighting and all going on, them colored people was celebrating. But not like they was doing in '35 when Joe Louis won his match against Carnera. No it was nothing compared to that. But it was still some celebration.

"The next day, after the all-night-long parties, some smart-ass little colored boy by the name of Open Mouth Rainey got shot to death in the Silver Dollar Bar and Grill. It seems this guy, Open Mouth, strolled into the restaurant and asked the owner for a cup of coffee as strong as Jack Johnson, and a steak beat up like Jim Jeffries. When he said that, the owner slapped him, reaching quickly for his six-shooter which was right under the counter. Open Mouth Rainey pulled his forty-four, but it was too late. The man had gotten the drop on Open Mouth. He burned him five times. Open Mouth barely had a chance. Let me tell you: Some of them crackers was sure mad that a nigger was now the heavyweight champion of the world.

"But the colored knew that it was quite natural for there to be a black champion. Since we was the first boxers in this country anyway. You see, Larry, boxing started out in Virginia. There it was the custom for the sons of aristocratic families to go to England where they received a first-rate education in the humanities. Also, while there, they were supposed to acquire the finer virtues by circulating among and socializing with the English gentry. Now along with education of the mind went the education of the body. Therefore, they were trained in the manly art of boxing. Now these scions of Southern aristocracy returned home from England with a good education and a knowledge of the rudiments of boxing. Back home, they started training some of the young slaves to be boxers. So they held contests among the slaves from different plantations.

"Pugilism, as it relates to us, son, got its formal start, however, with the career of one Tom Molyneaux. Mr. Molyneaux was the first colored champion. He was born in Virginia, a slave; and when he was, through some mysterious process, granted his freedom, he traveled to New York. By then, he had beaten everybody around, both Negroes and whites. Then he went to England to fight Tom Cribb who was then the world champion. This fight took place in December of 1810; I forget the exact date. But it was at Capthall Common in Sussex. These were the days before the Queensberry rules. As I recall, it was a dreary day, the fight lasted forty rounds. Tom Cribb won, but a lots of folks, particularly a guy they called West Indian Charlie, protested that there was tricknology involved in Cribb's victory. But be that as it may, that's how the colored got into boxing.

"All of the plantation owners, from all points, used to gather at their respective plantations to place wagers on one slave or the other. These men were all gentlemen, fine education, breeding, and plenty of money. So in many ways, they didn't care who really won the fight. It was all just considered good sport. They liked the way them niggers circled each other and doing them fancy steps, and dropping them bombs and do. Naturally, they got specially excited when one of them fellers drew blood. I once saw two slaves beat each other to death."

"It is late in the afternoon, sun swarming all over us. I am inside of a bull of a man named Silas. Amos swings a wild right at me. I block it easily, but he catches me with a left hook. It seems like all day we have been fighting like this. My arms and his arms are heavy, but we smash at each other and at the white blurry faces surrounding us. We go on like this until the sun begins going down. . . . The shouting and the rooting has died down now; now we lean on each other breathing hard and tied up in sweat like wrestlers. The contest has boiled down to grunts and awkward swings. . . . As darkness comes, we are both still standing. Judge Tate calls it a tie. They throw me in the buckboard, and carry me back to the plantation."

"You got the right idea, son. That's almost exactly how it was in those days. Yeah, that's just the way it went down. Them folks really liked the sports. And since they had lots of money, and not much to do, they just gambles all the time.

"Yes siree, them folks liked the sports and the sporting houses too. And I'm sure you know that they had betting tables in them houses too. An ex-boxer by the name of Bill Richmond ran one of the biggest whore houses in the city of New Orleans; but even though he himself was colored, he didn't allow no colored in there—'cept them girls he had working for him.

"I told you I used to be a boxer before I went to Stall's Minstrels. Woody Johnson was manager (may he rest in peace). I was swift and dancy, in the bantamweight class, like Eligio Sardinas who was otherwise known as "Kid Chocolate." I had me a pretty snappy jab, and my left hook was a monster. I got tired of the fight game though. And then I decided to go into show business? Why? 'Cause there was some very nice people in the business in those days, real educated and refined people like J. Rosamund Johnson. And I wanted to be one of them. So I gave up the fight game, even though I was good. In my time, I was on good terms with boxers like Battling Siki, Tiger Flowers, Joe Gans, Sammy the Smasher and Sam Langford. Me and Sam used to party a lot together. I'm not just name-dropping, son; I'm simply giving you my credentials so you will fully appreciate the facts I'm about to give you concerning the squared circle.

"A lots of black guys started hanging round the sporting events. In those days, we refered to these guys as the Sporting Crowd; or we called them Sports for short. Now all these sportsmens was fast livers. They dressed in the latest fashions, and wore finely tailored suits. Jelly Roll Morton used to hang around with that bunch quite often. Jelly Roll was the real sporting type. He played a wicked piano, was a ladies' man, spoke French, and had him a diamond ring on every finger. He even had a diamond in his middle tooth. You was liable to see old Jelly Roll anywhere and with anybody. He was around boxers and jockeys as much as he was round musicians.

"Well, now that we're talking about Jelly Roll, this brings me to the part of my discussion about boxing in general, and the Ali-Frazier fight in particular. Did you know that there is a distinct connection between boxing and music? You say you didn't know that? Well, there is. You see it's like this: Boxing is just another kind of rhythm activity. Like all sports is based on rhythm. Dig: If you ain't got no rhythm, you can't play no sports. Like jumping rope ain't nothing but dancing. Beating on the punching bag is the same as beating on drums. Everything connected with sports is connected with rhythm. You just think about it for a while. Every fighter has his own particular rhythmic style just the way musicians do. You ever notice that some fighters dance around a lot, doing fast rhythms; while some other guy is slower, likes to do the slow drag instead of the Lindy Hop or the jitterbug. Yes, Larry, this is so with all of its possible variations.

"All sports are just expressions of a particular attitude toward rhythm. But boxing unlike many other sports confines the players to a very small area of confrontation. Boxers are contained within a square. And this makes for particular difficulties. But it also makes for the particular attraction to the sport. Most men can identify with the sport because most men, at one time or the other, have had to hold their hands up. But what about the square? What has it to do with the sport? Well, the square symbolizes a discrete universe. That is to say, it brings to bear upon the material universe a particular sense of order. All geometrical constructs do. For example, the triangle, the Trinity and other ternary clusters seem to represent spiritual dynamism. The circle, on the other hand, represents some aspect of infinity. Perhaps oneness in God. The square, in its quaternary aspect, appears to symbolize the material realm, or the rational intellect. There is a negative aspect to the square though. In some ways the square implies stasis, and even decadence. But regardless of all of these factors, the square is the context in which one fighter confronts another one.

"Here we are dealing with the underlying premises behind the sport. We could say something about ritual here, but that side of the street has already been covered in great detail by Mr. Jack Johnson in his autobiography. Instead here, we are discussing the metaphysics of geometrical and dynamic modality.

"Now there are several things that determine the winner of a fight, or any sporting context for that matter. But all of these things are essentially tied up with rhythm. Because even though there is an implied circle within the square (and naturally without the square), one rhythmically described by the fighters themselves, the square, in this connection, is the creation of a particular historical sensibility. This sensibility manifests itself in all spheres of life and art. We see it asserting itself in architecture, technology and sociopolitical theories. The circle, on the other hand, exists as an ever-evolving metaconstruct. The fighter's duty is to rhythmically discern the essential unity between the circle and the square.

"Take this Muhammad Ali, for example; he knows all about squares and circles 'cause he is a Muslim. And all of them folks knows all about things like that. Like 360° = Allah. That kind of thing. He even know about rhythm. I hear he's a poet. Rhythm concerns the modality of space, sound, motion, and existence. Both space and motion can be manipulated rhythmically. Existence can also be manipulated in like manner; but we'll deal with that some other time when we are discussing contests that involve more than four persons. If we went into that now, we would have to discuss history, and that bitch is not the subject of my discussion.

"All fighters must understand the principles of rhythmic modality. The fighter who best understands these principles will most likely win the contest. Again, young man, rhythm here refers to the duration and the structure of the contest, its interlocking spatial and dynamic relationships, the manner in which one proceeds to handle the space dominated by his body, and the body of his opponent. It also refers to the artistic or technical manipulation of the space encompassed by the square which these fools erroneously call the "ring." By the use of a calculus, therefore, we arrive at the conclusion that the Ali-Frazier fight was, in fact, a contest of essentially different attitudes toward music.

"This was the secret wisdom that Jelly Roll Morton passed on to boxers of the twenties. This principle was orally transmitted through a long line of boxers until it was momentarily obscured by Floyd Patterson who was the first Hamlet of the boxing profession.

"Now Ali understands these principles of rhythm and music. Theoretically, that's what's so sweet about him. You see, he believes in riffing. He certainly has got the body, the legs, and the mouth for it. But Frazier is somewhere else in the musical universe. Frazier is stomp-down blues, bacon, grits, and Sunday church. 'Course them Muslims is different. They don't be eating none of that hog. They say it ruin your brains. It didn't seem to do Frazier no harm though, 'cept he do seem a little slow with the rap sometimes. But Joe Louis, an Alabama boy, raised on blackstrap molasses, was slow with the rap too. And you know how mean he could be upon entering the squared circle. But Ali is body bebop, while Frazier is slow brooding blues with a gospel bearing. Ali understands the mysteries of the circles and the squares, the same as Sufi poets do. That is to say, Larry, the essential metaphysics of these forms, for him, a constant source of religious and intellectual meditation. Ali prays (does his salats) in quiet meditation. But most likely, Frazier wants to shout in church. However, Ali, as a Muslim intellectual, has been forced to suppress his gospel impulse. But he can't suppress it totally. You can still hear it in his voice when he speaks, or when he tries to sing. But blues and gospel ain't his thing. Frazier can't sing, but he sings better than Ali. And that's why Frazier won the fight.

"I don't mean that he outsung Ali during the fight. I mean, instead, that he sang his particular song better than Ali sang his. Old slow-blues, pork-eating Frazier is moody and relentless. He got plenty killer in him. But bebop body, your man, is the urbanized philosopher of the would-be righteous, the future shaper in many respects. However, he is a blase singer, having a tendency to sound-down mammy-loving country boys who lack causes, and who are grateful for any desperate break they can get. Boys like Frazier envision purple suits, full-length Russian sable, beige Eldoradoes, the perfumed cluster of female flesh, and triumphant kisses from the Sepia Queen.

"Ali envisions a Nation full of intricate order, like an interlocking network of squares and rectangles. He dreams of kissing the black stone of Mecca. No loose perfumed ladies there. Perhaps there, mosques fly as zones of ultimate righteousness. The Muslim women wear long dresses; they pursue long periods of silence as they sidestep sin, murmuring polite Koranic knowledge.

"Your problem, my boy, primarily concerns making both of them understand the implicit unity between the circle and the square. Using a variant of the calculus that we set up earlier, I would say, therefore, that Frazier needs Ali's squares, and Ali needs Frazier's circles. I can't see it no other way.

"The essential dynamics of the squared circle demand that each contestant really understand how he sings best. That he choreograph and orchestrate his game in terms of what he does best. Theoretically, everyone in the sporting game knows this. But the pragmatics or translation of this abstract knowledge often eludes us. In the case of the particular spectacle under discussion, the fighters were very much evenly matched. They just simply manifested different choreographic styles. But given the pressure of the evening, its particular psychological atmosphere, its forced political overtone, the winner would be the one who most acutely understood the principles of spatial and psychic rhythm. Ali's science was winning until the first stunning blow caught him somewhere around the eighth round. (Note the quaternity of the number eight: 8.) But Ali also had not paced himself properly from the beginning of the match. He allowed himself to enter Frazier's system of deceptive choreography; a system full of treacherous memories that lay in the cut ready to pummel that bebopping body of his. The way to fight slow grinding powerhouses like Frazier is to not let them touch you at all—if it's humanly possible. Because, beneath that dull rap, there is a mad churning engine. And you have got to respect that kind of power." He looked at his watch.

"How about one for the road?" I said.

"That's all right with me, but it has got to be a quickie. I'm supposed to meet this chippie in a little while."

When the next round of drinks came, I toasted him and thanked him for his time. "Wow! Uncle Rufus, all that time you was talking you never told me who you were pulling for."

He looked at me long and hard. Then his black face broke into sarcastic smile. He reached down beneath the bar stool, and pulled his cane out. He held it up so that the golden-headed serpent would glitter as it caught the low amber light of the My Bar sign. He looked at the cane, and then at me. I could see now, looking at him full in the face, that he was really much older than he seemed. I saw the cane swiftly fly back. Before I had time to react, Uncle Rufus had whacked me hard across my arm.

"What was that about?" I whined, rubbing my aching arm.

"It's about you not learning to ask the right questions, especially after I done took all this time explaining things to you. Sheet! I really shouldn't give you no answer. But since you once told me you wanted to be a boxer, here it is: I was pulling for both of them. But this time, your old uncle put his money on slow blues. . . ."

1972

The Ethos of the Blues

*It's the mood. . . . That's the carry-over from slavery—
nothing but trouble in sight for everyone. There was
no need to hitch your wagon to a star because there
wasn't any stars. You got only what you fought for.
Spirituals were the natural release—"Times gonna
get better in de promised land"--but many a steve-
dore knew only too well that his fate was definitely
tied up in his own hands. If he was clever and
strong, and didn't mind dying, he came through—
the weak ones always died. A blue mood—since
prayers often seemed futile the words were made to
fit present situations that were much more real and
certainly more urgent.*
—Clarence Williams talking to E. Simms Campbell,
   in *Jazzmen*

This "mood" to which Clarence Williams refers is the characteristic personality or ethos that informs the spirituals and the
gospel songs. This "mood" or mode is the emotional archetype
from which the blues spring. The blues, with all of their
contradictions, represent, for better or for worse, the essential
vector of the Afro-American sensibility and identity. Berthing
themselves sometime between the end of formal slavery and the
turn of the century, the blues represent the ex-slave's confrontation with a more secular evaluation of the world. They were
shaped in the context of social and political oppression, but
they do *not*, as Maulana Karenga said, *collectively* "teach

107

resignation." To hear the blues in this manner is to totally misunderstand the essential function of the blues, because the blues are basically defiant in their attitude toward life. They are about survival on the meanest, most gut level of human existence. They are, therefore, lyric responses to the facts of life. The essential motive behind the best blues song is the acquisition of insight, wisdom.

Now the spirituals and the gospels are obviously concerned with moral wisdom, but encounter here takes place against a specific symbolic text, i.e., the Bible and its attendant folklore; while, for the blues singer, the world is his text. In the social sense, therefore, we sometimes find an implicit between gospel people and blues people. In some parts of the South, the known blues singer was often not even welcomed in the church. This is ironic since both forms of music spring from the same aesthetic, and also, there is no disputing the number of popular blues-oriented singers who had their apprenticeship in the church.

What we have here is not merely a social dichotomy along simplistic tribal lines, but different metaphysical attitudes toward existence. The blues impulse was very early associated with the more sinister aspects of life. It was perceived as springing from a deep dark place within the black ethos. Here, Dude Botley talks about Buddy Bolden, who in the historiography of the music, is seen as the major synthesizing agent—i.e., legend has it that he was one of the first to infuse the voice of the blues into the European horn:

> And I got to thinking about how many thousands of people Bolden had made happy and all them women who used to idolize him and them supposed to be friends. Where are they now? I say to myself. Then I hear Bolden's cornet. I look through the crack (in door) and there he is, *relaxed* back in the chair, blowing that silver cornet *softly,* just above a *whisper,* and I see he's got his hat over the bell of the horn. I put my ear close to the keyhole. I thought I had heard Bolden play the *blues* before, and play the *hymns* at *funerals,* but what he is playing now is *real strange* and I listen carefully, because he's playing something that, for a while sounds like the blues,

then like a hymn. I cannot make out the tune, but after a while I catch on. He is *mixing* up the blues with the hymns. He plays the blues *real* sad and the hymn sadder than the blues and then the blues sadder than the hymn. That is the first time that I had ever heard hymns and blues cooked up together. Strange cold feeling comes over me: *I get sort of scared because I know the Lord don't like that mixing the Devil's music with his music.* But I still listen because the music sounds so strange and I am sort of hypnotized. I close my eyes, and *when he blows the blues I picture Lincoln Park with all them sinners and whores shaking and belly rubbing. Then, as he blows the hymn, I picture my mother's church on Sunday, and everybody humming with the choir.* The picture in my mind kept changing with the music as he blew. It sounded like a *battle between the Good Lord and the Devil.* Something tells me to listen and see who wins. If he stops on the blues, the Devil wins.

Obviously, the two modes of musical expression are seen as antithetical to each other. I am sure that some of the readers remember how adamantly the late Mahalia Jackson refused to sing the blues. The blues undoubtedly owe something to that sense of body reality depicted in Botley's description of the "sinners" in Lincoln Park. For is not the "shaking and belly rubbing" finally the expression of the larger will to survive—to feel life in one's innermost being, even though it takes place in an oppressive political context?

Consider, for example, the manner in which Afro-Americans use the word "mean" to describe a piece of music: "Monk's solo was *mean*," or "Trane blows a *mean* horn." What about the expression "mean and evil" which we often find in the blues? And could the "Devil" in Dude Botley's description of the Bolden solo symbolize not the Christian Satan, but a cluster of deeply felt emotional experiences that manifest themselves in the ethos and the aesthetic of the blues? Therefore, Dude Botley gives us two kinds of ritual. One is secular and African—"shaking and belly rubbing"—the other is institutionalized ritual—his mother's church where "everybody" is humming. Two forms of ritual, one associated with acceptance of the ways of the Hebrew Jesus, i.e., the Lamb of God. The other ritual, on the outside of the church, in the green park, stands in opposition to the value system of Christianity. There are obviously contending angels here. The Blues Spirit, the dark angel of the African voice is in a tug-of-war for Bolden's soul with the white voice of the Christian missionaries. To be "mean" in the lexicon of the blues is to express one's emotional experiences in the most profound, most intense manner possible. It means daring to be, to feel, to see.

The ex-slave questions the morality and religion of the overall white society. This was a natural reaction to the world he saw around him. It was a place of torture and pain. But the world is also a place of wonder and encounter. Occasionally, one glimpsed some promise. But the immediate circumstances of one's life was often at odds with any of the idealistic aspirations outlined again and again in the spirituals. Therefore, although the blues are an extension of emotional and tonal qualities inherent in the spirituals, their chief emphasis is on the material world— the world as flesh, money, survival, freedom, lost love, unrequited love, and instable love. The emergence of the blues marks the important stage of the Afro-American musical identity.

In simplistic dialectical terms, the spirituals stand for one level of ritual consciousness—the blues for another. Both forms are primarily fundamental types of folk poetry. For example, the emphasis in blues songs is on the immediacy of life, the nature of man, and human survival in all of its physical and psychological manifestations. The blues are informed by a social history of mental and physical hardships; they lyrically address themselves to concrete life situations. And if life is perceived to be a battle of the sexes, or a quest for pleasure, that's just the way it is. The blues singer, acting as ritual poet, merely reflects the horrible and beautiful realities of life. He didn't make it that way, that is just the way things are. Hardships can conquer you, or you can conquer them. Therefore, toughness of spirit is an essential aspect of the ethos of the blues.

An ideal approach to the blues would be that of seeing them as an extensive body of folk literature, and therefore subject to all of the laws of folklore. That means where we have a variety of primary sources. The blues should be categorized according to subject matter (content), lyric and musical structure, style, region of origin and probable audience. There have been extensive field recordings of some of the earlier blues, but there does not appear to have been a conscientious attempt to systematize even these. Paul Oliver's study *Blues Fell This Morning* comes close, but more work is needed. The blues have their roots in the oral literature of black America; and a careful analysis of them as Oliver, Jones and Kiel have observed would reveal some very essential things about the Afro-American ethos.

No one has been able to ascertain precisely in what Southern localities the blues were born. Several writers have placed their origins in Mississippi or Alabama, but dating the origins of oral material is a difficult task. Blues songs could have had an "underground" existence anytime between 1860 and 1900. This is often the case with material which a folk population considers illicit or sinful, and as we have noted the blues were considered sinful songs by religious black folks. Therefore, it is highly possible that no white collector heard any such songs until they were popularized by W. C. Handy in 1912. It was not until about 1920 that serious study was devoted to the blues.

Handy's most famous piece of music was "Saint Louis Blues" which was originally refused by the publishers. Handy then set up his own company and published the song himself. ("Saint Louis Blues" is one of the world's best-known songs; but, strictly speaking, it is not a blues in the technical sense of the word. That is because it slightly alters the character and form of blues by the addition of a very pronounced tango rhythm. However, the song is fundamentally rooted in the blues tradition. It has a blues orientation and the general organization of its images is the same as that found in the blues.) By 1920 record companies were turning out a great deal of blues recordings directed at what the industry called the "race trade." But chances of examining the blues in their natural environment had somewhat diminished by then. The "devil songs," as religious black people called the blues, had become an integral part of the American music scene. If the early scholars of Afro-American music had been black men, and had not perhaps been so puritanical, our knowledge of the folk origins of the blues would not be so theoretical.

By the time the first blues, Hart Wand's *Dallas Blues*, was published in 1912, the migratory process which had helped to disperse the blues had been well under way. The songs were popping up in minstrel and vaudeville shows throughout the South. Itinerant troubadours were singing them in dance halls, cotton fields, whore houses, turpentine camps, and barrooms. The country blues singers were already stamped in the eyes of the black community as men of sin. Many Negro ministers warned their congregations against associating with blues singers. A black man traveling with a guitar ("devil box") was not allowed to pass even into the front yard of the church unless he left his guitar outside.

The social impulse in the blues, its raw quality, is almost completely at odds with the moral attitudes which the Negro ministers attempted to instill in the religious community. The music had arisen out of the same feeling which produced the spirituals, jubilees, gospel songs, and work songs. But the overt literary content of the blues was radically different from the view of the world as expressed in the spirituals.

To the blues singer the spirituals, finally, were the expression of beliefs not grounded in pressing reality. The blues are primarily the expression of a postslavery view of the world. They are linked to a freeing of the individual spirit. Slavery leans toward obliterating the individual's sense of *himself* as a person with particular needs and a particular style or manner of doing things. Every aspect of one's life is controlled from the outside by others, and the sense of one's individual body is diminished. It follows then, that the intensely *personal* quality of the blues is a direct result of freeing the individual personality which was often held in check by slavery. The ex-slave, therefore, accepted the Western concept of man. What other concept did he know? And furthermore, as Albert Murray observed in *The Omni-Americans*, "they were slaves who were living in the presence of more human freedom and individual opportunity than they or anybody else had ever seen before." The end of formal slavery would therefore alter the slave's horizon of experience. He would have to confront his own name. He would have to accept the fact that his life was in his own hands in a more immediately physical manner. He had seen slavery and survived it, and he wasn't going to be anybody's slave again. Herein would reside his essential strengths and contradictions for the political activists who would later try to organize him. Imamu Baraka explains this development in the following manner:

> But the insistence of blues verse on the life of the individual and his individual trials and successes on the earth is a manifestation of the whole Western concept of man's life, and it is a development that could only be found in an American black man's music. From the American black leader's acceptance of Adam Smith's *laissez faire* social inferences to some less fortunate black man's relegation to a lonely path of useless earth in South Carolina, the weight of Western tradition, or to make it more specific and local, the weight of just what social circumstances and accident came together to produce the America that the Negro was part of, had to make itself part of his life as well.

What the ex-slave, in fact, did was to adopt one of the main tenets of the democratic American ideal. His adoption of the philosophy of rugged individualism was a natural outgrowth of once having had his individual liberty curtailed. It was not necessarily an attempt to succeed in terms of capitalist ideals. This was to come later with the rise of the Negro bourgoisie.

The blues are the ideology of the field slave—the ideology of a new "proletariat" searching for a means of judging the world. Therefore, even though the blues are cast in highly personal terms, they stand for the collective sensibility of a people at particular stages of cultural, social, and political development. The blues singer is not an alienated artist attempting to impose his view of the world on others. His ideas are the reflection of an unstated general point of view. Even though he is a part of the secular community, his message is often ritualistic and spiritual. Therefore, it is his ritual role in the community which links him to the traditional priests and poets of Africa.

And ironically enough, a cursory examination of the lives of many ritual artists everywhere in the world. Let us keep in mind, therefore, that the blues are primarily folk expression. Consequently, they are subject to the processes of myth and ritual out of which all folklore is derived. Ralph Ellison makes a similar point in a review of Baraka's *Blues People*:

> Classic blues were both entertainment *and* a form of folklore. When they were sung professionally in theatres, they were entertainment, when danced to in the form of recordings or used as a means of transmitting the traditional verses and their wisdom, they were folklore. There are levels of time and function involved here, and the blues which might be used in our place as entertainment (as gospel music is now being used in night clubs and on theatre stages) might be put to a ritual use in another. Bessie Smith might have been a "blues queen" to the society at large, but within the tighter Negro community where the blues were part of a total way of life, and a major expression of an attitude toward life, she was a priestess, a celebrant who affirmed the values of the group and man's ability to deal with chaos.

Like any artist, the blues singer has the task of bringing order out of chaos. The songs he sings, whether his own creations or others', are reenactments of his life and the lives of his people. The immediate emotional projections of what he has seen and felt are certainly personal, but they never remain simply that. Because they are in reality only symbolic of the larger human dilemma:

> There's several types of blues—there's blues that connects you with personal life—you can tell it to the public as a song. But I mean, they don't take seriously what you are tellin' the truth about. At the same time it could be you, more or less it *would* be you for you to have the feelin'. You express yourself in a song like that. *Now this particular thing reaches others because they have experienced the same condition in life, so naturally they feel what you are sayin' because it happened to them* [Emphasis mine].

It's a sort of thing that you kinda like to hold to yourself, yet you want somebody to know it. I don't know how you say that two ways: you like somebody to know it, yet you hold it to yourself. Now I've had the feelin' which I have disposed it in a song, but there's somethings that have happened to me that I wouldn't dare tell, not to tell—but I would *sing* about them. Because people in general they takes the song as an explanation for *themselves*—they believe this song is expressing *their* feelin's instead of the one that singin' it. They feel that maybe I have just hit upon somethin' that's their lives, and yet at the same time it was some of the things that went wrong with me too.

The singer is aware that his audience has been through the same changes as he has. His task is to express through his craft their suffering and his. Everything and everyone who he encounters on his journey of the soul is mirrored in his art. He is appreciated as a meaningful member of the community to the degree to which he expresses the conscious and unconscious spirit of that community. Therefore, the blues singer should not be viewed apart from the community ethos that produced him. He is a product of a long chain of historical and social events. The blues people, as Imamu Amiri Baraka calls them, are really the true heroes and poets of the community because they are able to reveal the essential essence of human experiences. In this sense they are as spiritually dedicated to their tasks as any minister or social revolutionary. Here is John Lee Hooker, one of the best known of the country blues singers speaking on the role of the singer. He is speaking to a concert audience at the Newport Jazz Festival:

> To you and all of my friends . . . especially my fellow mens, I'm so glad that we're here. . . . It's a big wide world . . . We come a long ways . . . We trying to throw a program, me, Brownie [McGhee], Sonny [Terry], everybody . . . all folksingers. We are here to pay our dues to the natural facts. You know . . . we have come a long ways . . . we all . . . we entertainers trying to reach you to bring you the message

of the blues . . . and folk. Sometimes we traveling
late at night. We are trying to reach you . . . to pay
our dues to the natural facts . . . to you, for your
enjoyment. All entertainers . . . Sometimes . . . you
tired when you reach your destination. But you're
paying your dues to the facts. But we are here to
please you the best way we know. I hope you
accept . . . Thanks.

Hooker gives this monologue running short riffs on his guitar. Each riff is a comment on his verbal statements, and a
kind of musical extension of the ideas he is trying to present to
his audience. The key phrases in this monologue refer to "paying
dues," bringing "the natural facts," "trying to reach you," and
bringing "the messages of the blues."

"Paying dues" is an expression quite common in the black
community. Roughly, it means that an individual has under-
gone a great many emotional and physical catastrophies, and
that he has, somehow, overcome them. Paying one's dues could
mean anything from losing your woman to having been in jail
all of one's life. It is a highly important group value, and there
is almost a religious attitude about it. The same is true for
telling the "natural facts." Note that the facts are *natural*;
earth-centered, rather than focused on some metaphysical realm.
And there is an obvious didactic reason for conveying these
"natural facts."

The didactic and moralistic impulse underlying the blues is
often obscured by the fact that many blues songs seem to be
inordinately concerned with the sex act: the constant allusions
to "jellyroll" and "cake" for example. It also is true that the
sexual content of the blues has been exploited by the record
industry. The high preponderance of blues songs dealing with
the sex act, apart from any reasons integral to the song itself, may
stem from the tendency of some blues singers to give the record
companies a great amount of marketable materials. However,
any extensive survey of the blues indicates that they cover a
broad range of subject matter. In the most meaningful blues, sex
fits neatly into the overall meaning of the song. Even in the most
salacious of blues songs, however, the import is still didactic:
Here is Eugene Rhodes's version of Josh White's *Jelly, Jelly*:

Hello, baby, I had to call you on the phone,
Hello, baby, I had to call you on the phone,
Yes, I'm so sad and lonely, need the baby home.
Downright rotten, lowdown dirty shame,
Downright rotten, lowdown dirty shame,
Way you treat me, woman; know I'm not to blame.
Jelly, jelly, jelly, jelly stays on my mind,
Jelly, jelly, jelly, jelly stays on my mind,
Jellyroll killed my mother, ran my daddy stone blind.

The blues are not concerned with middle-class morality, black or white. That is because the audience that they address is forced to confront the world of the flesh: the body is real, the source of much joy and pain. There is very little attempt to euphemize the realities of male-female relationships. It is the evangelical mind that often rejects these realities, that are appalled by the fleshy reality of the blues. Tin Pan Alley popular songs sing of "making whoopee," or "making love." The blues singer exclaims, "My man, he rocks me with one steady roll." Bessie Smith sings: "He's a deep sea diver with a stroke that can't go wrong." Certainly, these lines show more appreciation of the sex act than that of "making whoopee" or "making love." They are certainly more poetic. They celebrate the sex act in the fullest, most complete manner. The blues sing the joys and the pain of the world of flesh, while the pop songs of America rehash the dullness of a dying society.

The ethos of the blues, then, is the musical manifestation of one's individual cultural experiences in Afro-America with which members of the black community can identify. The blues performer has a talk with himself about the problem, analyzes the situation, and then takes his own advice to remedy it. He thereby opens up his soul to the world and allows it to see the sadness, the heartache, and the joys he has sustained in life—the trials and tribulations that get him down, but nevertheless, his determination to "make it"—and if he can get a witness, someone who can testify to the same feelings and experiences, then he has succeeded in revealing the essential essence of human experiences.

1971

My Lord, He Calls Me by the Thunder

Today we are all in the process of reexamining Western value systems. I speak specifically of the black political activist, artist, writer, or system builder. Anyone who is serious about liberation for black people is somehow engaged in the task of evaluating those aspects of our national life which make us who we are. This is correct, and necessary. But I would only hope that in our zeal to reach deeper levels of spiritual and political fulfillment, we do not attempt to deny totally the essential aspects of our group ethos.

We talk of building a Nation, a Nation either of the mind or of some definite physical space. But that Nation can only be the final cohesion of all of its operable parts into a collective sensibility. Therefore, it is the job of the system builders—whether they are ministers, politicians, artists or engineers—to glean from the whole of our experiences those values and practices that beyond all others have enabled us to survive spiritually. The black church, for instance, is a definite factor in the survival of a black ethos here in North America:

This fact is often overlooked by many of us because we are often insecure in our newfound consciousness. Insecurity frequently leads us to conclude, falsely, that all of our problems would be solved if the Black masses would only convert to some specific ideological or theological tenets—namely, the ones we adhere to. But in reality, the problem is far more complex than any one ideological position because life itself is essentially fluid and changing. The problem is further compounded by the propensity of young black people to perceive

118

the current struggle for national self-determination in limited terms. Some militants write and act as if there had been no real attempts at black liberation until Willie Ricks and Stokely Carmichael shouted, "Black Power!" on the Meredith March. Since we believe that we are the generation that started the proverbial ball rolling, we tend to view much of our history in a purely negative light.

There are, for example, black poets who speak of black people as "spiritually dead." Such thinkers, in their urge to develop new values for the Nation, are rejecting those aspects of the black culture experience that would truly constitute the stuff of Nationhood.

Thus, Christianity comes under vicious attack. We find ourselves accepting the myth of the black church as the "opiate of the people." The church is viewed as the great brainwasher of black people and the tool of the oppressors. We accept negative aspects of the folklore surrounding the black church, but we fail to probe the origins of this folklore.

Meanwhile, millions of black people continue to support their local churches, and to build new ones. In other words, a life-style exists among black folk that is totally at odds with the attitudes of nationalist intellectuals who instead of denigrating the religion of much of the national black body should be trying to understand the influence—past and present—of the black church. In short, these intellectuals often look down on their mothers and fathers whose spiritual legacy gave birth to the very struggle we all claim to support. I believe nationalism is the central mode of black liberation. But nationalism can also fail if it doesn't unite all of the relevant parts of our entire experience.

Yes, it's true that Christianity was a tool of white oppression. Any religion if it teaches submission to oppression is antihuman. But that doesn't really tell us anything. Under colonialism, all institutions can, in fact, function as instruments of oppression. The church is of special importance because it purports to minister to the spiritual needs of its followers. It claims to be the hot line between God and Man. Consequently, religion impinges upon the most guarded areas of man's psyche. And in the case of the African man, religion occupies a central place in his existence.

Under slavery, the collective practice of non-Christian religions was forbidden. All of this is well known. But what seems to be forgotten by the proselytizing activist is that instead of being overwhelmed by Western Christianity, black people brought to it a totally different sensibility. And along with this new sensibility they injected into it a dynamic set of values—values that finally sought to transcend Christianity itself.

Of prime importance was the African's attitude toward God. In black church sermon and song God is personal, someone you might know, an integral part of life. He is certainly more clearly delineated than the European God or the Hebrew Yahweh of the Old Testament. Moreover, in a current song by The Edwin Hawkins Singers, His son, Jesus, is referred to as a "lover of my soul." So even though both Europeans and Christian Africans based their religious services on the Bible, the enslaved Africans were the only North American people to glean from the Bible an original literature, music, and preaching style. It is, therefore, the black church that becomes the primary source for the subsequent development of all the important strands of black music. At the base of the music of Aretha Franklin, James Brown, John Coltrane, and Pharoah Sanders is the black gospel song and sermon. Even though at its roots religious black music is Eastern not Western, it was in the West, not the East, that we saw the fullest flowering of the black voice. Christianity, like everything else the black man has touched in the West, has been transformed by the African presence.

But the black church and its history are full of contradictions. Chief among them is the fact that many slaves knew, in very certain terms, that the Christianity practiced by the white slaver was oppressive. But still they felt that it was necessary to worship God in any manner sanctioned by white laws. Here is one slave's account of a typical sermon by a white minister:

> The niggers didn't go to the church building; the preacher preached to them in their quarters. He'd just say "serve your masters. Don't steal your master's turkey. Don't steal your master's chickens. Don't steal your master's hogs. Don't steal your master's meat. Do whatsoever [sic] your master tells you to do." Same old thing all the time. (B. A. Botkin, *Lay My Burden Down*)

This happens to a captive people, especially when propaganda is backed by obviously superior military force. In such a state, the natural urge for survival motivates people to pretend to go along with a con game. They appear to be acting out their roles as defined by the oppressor. But internally they are about something else. They have wills of their own, an interior world that is private, belonging to them alone. This is something that cannot be denied people, even though the external oppression may be of awesome dimensions. And in their private consciences black people were able to distinguish between truth and falsehood, sincerity and insincerity, between their own interests and the interests of the slave establishment:

> One time when an old white man came along who wanted to preach, the white people gave him a chance to preach to the niggers. The substance of his sermon was this· "Now when you servants are working for your masters you must be honest. When you go to the mill, don't carry along an extra sack and put some of the meal or flour in for yourself. And when you women are cooking in the big house, don't make a big pocket under your dress and put a sack of coffee and a sack of sugar and other things you want in it." They took him out and hanged him for corrupting the morals of the slaves. (B. A. Botkin, *Lay My Burden Down*)

Can you dig it? This attitude clearly illuminates an aspect of the group ethos masked in the language of innuendo, double-entendre, and trickery. All of these are the stratagems of an oppressed people trying to assert their own place and face in the world. A person holding these ideas could hardly have been brainwashed by Christianity, but that does not mean that such a person would reject the fundamentally sound morality of the Christian doctrine. And since Christianity was the only legally sanctioned religion, blacks were forced either to make Christianity indigenous to their lives or to take their African religions underground, as many of them did.

But it is the reconstruction of Christianity by the Black man that interests us here. Originally, black Christians were allowed to worship in the same churches as the white "brethren."

Sometimes they went to separate services. Sometimes they were confined to a certain section in the church. Frequently they were allowed to worship in their own places as long as a white person was present. On some plantations, slaves were not permitted to gather for fear they might plot an insurrection. (Remember that Nat Turner was a preacher who based his justification for rebellion on the Scriptures.) On others, the slaves had to conduct clandestine Afro-Christian services.

But it is important to understand that some kind of religious service had to be conducted. Why is this so? Because there is a clear spiritual impulse revealed in African culture. This impulse helped to sustain the African in the Western Hemisphere. It enabled him to shape the religions and the cultures of the conquering Europeans into forms that were compatible with his own sensibilities. The tragedy is that the transplanted African culture was never allowed to flower on its own terms. Therefore, for the Africans in America, the church became the instrument of their spiritual legacy.

Slaves who accepted Christianity adopted it fervently. If they judged the bosses in light of the professed principles of the church, they must surely have found in practice that the slave masters lacked any visible morality. To put it another way, if blacks had been allowed to read or have access to any of the Bible's most elementary truths, it would have become quite clear that white people were poor Christians, and that consequently they would suffer for it.

Black people worked hard at making Christianity a functional religion, something that white men apparently were not about to do. Many white ministers were often inveterate racists. Here is Jenny Proctor, a slave born in 1850, speaking:

> They [sic] wasn't no church for the slaves, but we goes to the white folks arbor on Sunday evening, and a white man he gits up there to preach to the niggers. He say, "Now I takes my text which is, Nigger obey your masters and your mistress, 'cause what you git from them here in this world am all you ever going to git, 'cause you just like the hogs and the other animals—when you dies you ain't no more, after you been throwed in that hole." I guess we

believed that for a while 'cause we didn't have no
way of finding out different. We didn't see no Bibles.

All of the remarks quoted here were made by slaves. They
were recorded in B. A. Botkin's *Lay My Burden Down: A Folk
History of Slavery*. Each account demonstrates how Christian
doctrine functioned as a tool of oppression. However, they do
indicate a kind of psychological separation between the African's idea of himself and God, even though they also substanti-
ate the nationalist contention that Christianity was a brutal
attempt to destroy the humanity of the slaves.

The ethics of white Christianity were constantly being tested
under slavery. For the most part, Christianity suffered from
the test. But black men found themselves in a dilemma. For a
number of legal and social reasons they were unable to practice
their traditional religions. Therefore they were forced to go to
the white church. Even there they found their humanity denied them. It was an awareness of these realities that finally led
to the building of a separate black church network.

It was after constant harassment whenever he tried to worship at the St. George Methodist Church in Philadelphia that
Richard Allen established the Bethel African Methodist Episcopal Church in 1787. This marked the origins of the black
church movement. Branches of Allen's church sprang up in
Baltimore and Wilmington, and in Pennsylvania and New Jersey towns. The black church, strengthened by this cooperation
among people, continued to expand after surviving a temporary
setback after the Denmark Vesey insurrection in 1822.

The black church not only survived, it became an integral
part of the community. In fact, it has been for years the only
tightly knit institution in the black community, and has come
to serve a wide variety of the community's needs. The black
church supplied us with our first crop of indigenous leaders,
educational institutions, publishing houses, insurance coopera-
tives, and burial societies. And the black church pioneered the
development of New York City's Harlem as a distinct cultural
community. The Abyssinian Baptist Church, St. Philip's Prot-
estant Episcopal Church, and St. Mark's Methodist Church
bought up large blocks of property from white landowners in
the twenties, thus meeting the urgent need for housing that

arose after the large influx of black people from the South. All
of this is not to deny the fact that some church leaders have
misdirected their congregations or that others have done very
little in the struggle for political liberation. But don't forget
that the current surge of national self-determination has very
often been sparked by black church leaders. The nationalist
system builders are going to have to reassess their attitudes
toward the church. They àre going to have to understand
precisely why this institution continues to serve as a wellspring
of energy and truth, in spite of the rapid changes in our
community.

One thing is certain. In spite of the turning toward African and
Eastern religions, there are millions of black people in America
who consider themselves Christians. These millions are not going
to make quick conversions to any current ideological trend,
however contemporary and relevant that trend seems to be;
nor is their faith going to disappear in the face of some vague
rhetoric. Furthermore, I am not quite sure that such a conver-
sion is even necessary or desirable. The black church, however, finds itself in the same position as the Algerian nationalists
who had to confront both the positive and negative tendencies in
Islam in order to unify national consciousness. The revolutionary
black churchman must take the implicit values of Christianity
and shape them according to the cultural needs of his people.

He must alter the racist symbology of the European Christian,
and propose a system of images that affirms the essential humanity
of his congregation. He must move, in his sphere, to sharpen
their social consciousness. He can do this better than most
activists because he commands a base of operations, while most
activists, however pertinent their ideas, don't control anything.

In the coming years, the black church will face a major
challenge. Young black people everywhere are demanding that
religion and education be relevant to the struggle. Black people will be undergoing far-reaching changes in religious attitudes.
These changes will parallel the rise in national consciousness.
The black church will either accommodate their changes, or
become an artifact of the past. But I don't believe the latter
will ever come about. I believe that we'll all be working together, building the Nation.

1970

On Malcolm X
from "New Space/The Growth of Black Consciousness in the Sixties"

What I liked most about Malcolm was his sense of poetry; his speech rhythms, and his cadences that seemed to spring from the universe of black music. Because I was not reared in the black church I was something of an anomaly among Northern blacks. I did not have ready access to the rhetorical strategies of Martin Luther King [, Jr.] My ears were more attuned to the music of urban black America––that blues idiom music called jazz. Malcolm was like that music. He reminded many of us of the music of Charlie Parker and John Coltrane—a music that was a central force in the emerging ethos of the black artistic consciousness. Malcolm was in the tough tradition of the urban street speaker. But there was a distinct art in his speeches, an interior logic that was highly compelling and resonant.

Malcolm X was assassinated on February 21, 1965, at the Audubon Ballroom in Upper Manhattan. It was a very un-February-like day; I recall a hot sun. The sister I was with was accompanied by her daughter, who was about twelve years old. We belonged to an organization that supported Malcolm after his break with the Black Muslims. The split began with Malcolm's statement that the Kennedy assassination was an example of "chickens coming home to roost." At the time, he asserted that the sins of white America had caused Allah to visit this calamity of the assassination on the country. But it was such a startling statement, made while the nation was still in mourning, that the Honorable Elijah Muhammad put Malcolm

125

on probation. He was forbidden from public speaking for three months. This was, in itself, quite a startling development because Malcolm was very popular in the Afro-American community at large.

Meanwhile, the Muslims were undergoing an internal struggle over the question of political activism. The Muslims generally existed outside of the civil rights struggle. They were strongly opposed to integration. They did not support any political movements outside of their structure. Malcolm, on the other hand, often addressed himself to struggles of the civil rights workers, particularly the so-called militant wing of the movement. He found himself drifting closer and closer to the nationalistic elements. He found himself speaking more and more about the murders and the beatings that some of the young organizers were experiencing in the South and in the urban communities of the North. He wanted the Nation of Islam to become more involved in the political struggle as activists, and not just as enlightened commentators on the side lines.

I lived on 105th Street off Central Park West then; so the three of us, I, Ahada, and her twelve-year-old daughter, Amina, headed for the Eighth Avenue local, which would take us to 165th Street where Broadway and St. Nicholas intersect. The Audubon Ballroom was opposite a small park. We carried bundles of our newspaper, *Black America,* to sell at the rally where Malcolm was speaking. We were a little late, which was bad. It meant that we'd missed the opportunity to sell the paper to the crowd that usually milled outside the auditorium before the rally. It was strange and eerie when we emerged from the subway at the park. Most of the time when Malcolm spoke at the ballroom there were policemen everywhere. But on this particular afternoon, nothing; just the weird February sun. We made our way up the stairs to the ballroom, and no one searched us at the door. That too was surprising. Inside, we quickly slid into one of the booths that surrounded the perimeter of the dance floor, near the back, on the left side of the aisle facing the stage. The meeting hadn't quite started.

It was the kind of Sunday that made church-going people put on their finest. There were flowered hats of all colors and descriptions. There were children too, a lot of children like Amina. Some of the women wore African head wraps, called *geles*. There was something churchlike about the whole ambience, but there wasn't any organ music to entertain this congregation as it fidgeted through a speech by Brother Benjamin X, which, if I recall, was about the liberation movements in Africa, Asia, and Latin America. Then he said the following: "And now, without further remarks, I present to you one who is willing to put himself on the line for you, a man who would give his life for—I want you to hear, listen, to understand—one who is a Trojan for the Black man!"

We responded, "Wa-laikum salaam."

We all knew that there had been several attempts on Malcolm's life. A premonition of impending violence passed over me. Guards moved into place. I remember thinking: If it's gonna happen, it's gonna happen now. The sun was shafting through the windows. The audience had quieted down in anticipation of Malcolm; and after what seemed like two or three long minutes Malcolm came out.

"As salaam alaikum, brothers and sisters."

"Wa-laikum salaam," we answered.

Count about ten beats, after the sound of the response dies down.

An obvious commotion had started down in the front rows. Malcolm was standing at a podium. He stepped from behind the podium to quiet the commotion. He said something like, "Peace, be cool, brothers." Then it came. The strongest possible message, direct. The shots came rapid fire. Malcolm fell back, his arms flung outward like wings from the impact of the bullets hitting him square in the chest. Then there was the rumbling of scuffling feet, and chairs were overturned. After it happened there seemed to be a pause, then the fear was everywhere. People scrambled for cover on the floor under the tables in the back, shouting. Screams came from the women and children. It seemed like the shots were coming from all over the ballroom (a smoke bomb in the rear, found later, didn't go off). Security guards were trying to reach Malcolm, trying to stop the assassins who now were safely escaping in the confusion. Ahada's daughter bolted out of the seat beside us. Ahada managed to catch the child before she could be trampled by the mob. A gunman ran by us, shooting and hurdling over chairs in his way. He twisted and turned, and fired at a knot of black men chasing him. The man was still firing as he ran out of the door toward the 165th Street entrance. He was being chased by several of Malcolm's men. They caught him at the top of the steps, and he was wounded in the thigh. Another assassin left by the side door, waving his gun, daring anyone to follow him. The whole room was a wailing woman. Men cried openly.

Malcolm's death was an awesome psychological setback to the nationalist and civil rights radicals. The established Negro leadership lamented his death, but qualified their lamentations by asserting that he "preached by the sword, now he has died by the sword." The militants and the nationalists, on the other hand, felt guilty. They felt that they had not done enough to support Malcolm while he was alive. Hence, they had not protected him, and, somehow, they felt responsible for his assassination. After all, had Malcolm not said that his life was in danger? Had not the man's home been bombed only a week before his assassination? How we gonna build anything if we let our leaders get shot down like dogs? We were ready to retaliate, but everything was fuzzy. The assassins were Negroes, and we really couldn't get that together. Malcolm had broken with the Muslims, and had previously accused them of trying to kill him. But we could not understand why the Muslims would want to kill Malcolm, considering that they would be the prime suspects. No, that didn't make sense.

We considered the CIA, the right wing, the Zionists, and the Mafia. Lacking facts and a clear orientation, we found these considerations merely led to interminable days of agonizing arguments, and charges, and countercharges.

But even though Malcolm's death—the manner of it—emotionally fractured young black radicals, there were two central facts that all factions of the movement came to understand. And they are: that the struggle for black self-determination had entered a serious, more profound stage; and that for most of us, nonviolence as a viable technique of social change had died with Malcolm on the stage of Audubon.

Some of us did not survive the assassination. Strain set in. Radical black organizations came under more and more official scrutiny, as the saying goes. The situation made everyone paranoid, and there were often good reasons for being so. People were being set up, framed on all kinds of conspiracy charges. There was a great deal of self-criticism, attempts to lock arms against the beast that we knew lurked outside.

Some people dropped out, rejecting organizational struggle altogether. Some ended up in hippie cults in the East Village. Some even started shooting smack again. Some joined the poverty program; some did serious work there, while others, disillusioned and, for now, weak, became corrupt poverticians.

Malcolm's organization, the Organization of Afro-American Unity (OAAU), after being taken over very briefly by Sister Ella Collins, Malcolm's sister, soon faded. But the ideas promulgated by Malcolm did not. Malcolm's ideas had touched all aspects of contemporary black nationalism: the relationship between black America and the Third World; the development of a black cultural thrust; the right of oppressed peoples to self-defense and armed struggle; the necessity of maintaining a strong moral force in the black community; the building of autonomous black institutions; and finally, the need for a black theory of social change.

After Malcolm's death, thousands of heretofore unorganized black students and activists became more radically politicized. The Black Arts Movement started in Harlem with the opening of Black Arts Repertory Theater School under the direction of Imamu Amiri Baraka (LeRoi Jones). The Black Arts school attempted to effect a union between art and politics. Not since the thirties had such a union been attempted with such intensity. Never before had black artists entered into such a conscious spiritual union of goal and purpose. For the first time in history there existed a "new" constellation of symbols and images around which to develop a group ethos. What was happening in Harlem was being repeated all over the United States. Black people were shaping a new concept of themselves both in the national and international sense. Where we were going, we did not know. But one thing was certain, we knew that, as James Brown says, we were a "New Breed." At first we were smug and self-righteous in this newfound knowledge of ourselves. We were often arrogant and pushy. Underneath these negatives, we knew that much of what we were about was concertedly related to the total liberation of black people. We knew that without a strong sense of nationalism black people would not survive America. There was no way to survive America fragmented and in general confusion about who we were, and what we wanted.

All of the development of our remembered and unremembered history began to weigh down on us. And the more of our memory that returned to us, the sharper, the more acute the pain became. The more we probed our history and the history of the Third World, the more angry we became, the more nourished our hate for the white world. It had to go down that way. There was a concrete historical reason for everything that we felt. White people deserved to be hated uncritically. Sometimes in our perception of them, they even ceased to be people. They were the "Big White Fog" of the Ted Ward play. They became like the snow falling in Richard Wright's *Native Son*—a dead natural phenomenon that contaminated the entire planet. We reversed the Manichean dualism that placed the symbolism of blackness on the side of Evil, and whiteness on the side of Good.

This was a necessary reversal. But it led to some contradictions, the most important of which was that our nationalism could not exist primarily in contradistinction to white nationalism. We could never hope to develop a viable concept of self if that concept were purely based on hating crackers. The primary focus of our emotional energies would have to be black people. If we made the mistake of constantly addressing scorn and venom to white people, we would fall into the moribund category of the Negro leaders who seemed to be constantly affirming the black man's humanity to white people, and thus constantly implying that somehow black people would gain their humanity when the benevolence of white people finally asserted itself.

It did not matter the style of the address. Even if it was one of scorn and vindication, or if, as in the case of James Baldwin, it was rooted in compassion and an ardent desire to make one's self felt as a human being, this approach still implicitly fortified the white man's sense of power in the world. We could historically trace this tendency among black leaders, a tendency that has blurred vision and shattered energies. We had to dig each other, for each other, on our own terms, and on the basis of the common emotional history that we shared; a history that had shaped us both positively and negatively. Somewhere in the maw of that history we will find the means of redeeming ourselves, of "vindicating the blues," as Askia [Toure] says. It had to be that way. Accepting this reality, we can now begin to deal from a strong emotional base.

We will take a stand in the history primarily on the basis of our own emotional history. We have become synthesizers, bringing to bear upon the struggle all of the accumulated knowledge of the world. We can only deal realistically if we know where we are coming from. So we got to start dealing with specifics, each to each. That's not an easy thing to do. Black people know how to relate to white people; that part of the survival kit is cooled out. But relating to each other, that's another thing. We have still to get that together. Witness our brothers in the Black Panthers struggling for liberalism like everybody else, but so caught up in addressing themselves to the white community that they, in spite of their deaths and harassments, have become objects of art for jaded folks like Leonard Bernstein and Mrs. Peter Duchin. "It's exciting," the bitch says. And all the time our brothers in the black berets know that it is not exciting. In fact, it's some rather serious shit. Even though it may have started as a dimly perceived game, when you get right down next to it, up under its skin, it ain't no game. No kind of way.

Cut loose from a unified center, we become freaks, confused, driven from without rather than from within. The Eunuch has found his balls only to become the object of wholesale masturbation. Revolution becomes a talk show, the maudlin chatterings of some Hollywood actor. You become just another object of glamour. Slick white boys manage your most private affairs. The swiftness that is you, your essence, becomes mechanized, a glib part of a dead game. Outside of the ethos, you have to become bitchy and perverted, 'cause you ain't holding on to nothing. You are being squeezed spermless, your seed scattered among the ice and rocks.

Think about a nation, a place where, as much as natural laws will allow, you can shape your face. Like:

visions/all forms/actual life is the poem
your song bodies/life faces
your face/your child's face
save something Brother/but let the dead thing go/
com' on now/shape the face/and space/yes Father
and space/yes/save space/give breath to words
make a world/com' on now/move/give fire to deeds
love your millions/make a place for all of the faces/
but mostly your own/be change/love no dead things
give flesh to energy/do it with style/nigger elegance/
com' on now Brother/shape a space/
love your face/make a place. . . .

Black Power in the International Context

The struggle for black liberation has come to a significant turning point. Currently, the most advanced elements of the Black Power movement are beginning to understand the international implications of the struggle of black liberation. It is becoming increasingly clear that the struggle cannot be contained within the bounds of national life. As a matter of fact to continue to do so is a tendency that must be strongly fought. The African-American struggle is inextricably linked to the worldwide struggles of oppressed peoples against decadent political and economic systems.

The present-day attempts to put the struggle on an international basis have their roots in the writings of such nineteenth-century thinkers as Martin R. Delany who was the first Afro-American to raise the question of self-determination for the Africans. In the twentieth century, Garvey, DuBois, Malcolm X, and Harold Cruse have examined the relationship between the Afro-American struggle and the international situation in more precise details.

During the twenties, Garvey used Delany's slogan "Africa for the Africans" as the rallying cry for the United Negro Improvement Association. DeBois wrote in *The Souls of Black Folk*: "The problem of the twentieth century is the problem of the color line—the relation of the darker to the lighter races of men in Asia and Africa, the Americas, and the islands of the seas." Malcolm X, extracting from both Garvey and DuBois, constantly urged the movement to internationalize itself.

Therefore, the current internationalist tendencies of groups like SNCC, CORE, and RAM [Revolutionary Action Movement] should not come as a surprise. They are perfectly consistent, given an understanding of the history of the black man's struggle in America. The present movement is part of a historical process that began with Garvey and the NAACP. It was Garvey who first posed a concrete threat to European colonial interests in Africa. And it was the NAACP, under DuBois's direction, which established a viable Pan-Africanism—a Pan-Africanism which greatly influenced nationalist leaders like Dr. Kwame Nkrumah and Jomo Kenyatta. As late as 1949, the NAACP was supporting wars of national liberation:

> We stretch our hand across the sea to the new independent state of India. We hail the Indonesians in their struggle for liberty. We are one with the Africans in their effort to throw off the yoke of colonialism. We offer them every assistance within our power. The race problem is bigger than the few prejudiced men who influence the United States Congress. It is bigger than a few states in the deep South. It has assumed world-wide proportions and the American Negro is prepared to take his place in the world-wide struggle.

This statement was made by Roy Wilkins at the fortieth annual convention of the NAACP on July 12, 1949. Wilkins's statement is essentially a reworking of DuBois's remarks concerning the color question in *The Souls of Black Folk*. Since then Roy Wilkins has tended to de-emphasize the international role of the NAACP. This de-emphasis is directly related to the general manner in which the NAACP has now come to see the struggle in this country.

The main thrust of the NAACP is now directed toward assimilating blacks into the present socio-economic structure of white America. But in the present political and economic context this is neither possible nor desirable. On the national level, it means the destruction of potential pockets of black resistance to white America's decadent political structure. On the international level, it means that black America becomes aligned with the racist power structure in the destruction of the Third World (Africa, Asia, and Latin America). Therefore, the

NAACP and similarly oriented Negro leaders display strong acceptance of United States foreign policy. And American foreign policy is essentially reactionary.

Consequently, one of the things separating Black Power militants from the traditional wing of the movement is a basic difference in the way history is viewed. Roy Wilkins and Whitney Young are both descended from slaves, as were Malcolm X and Marcus Garvey. But there are profound differences in orientation between these two groups of men. Their political orientations undoubtedly play a role in their style of action. Whitney Young would not act like Malcolm because Malcolm's assessment of the world and Young's are vastly different. Young's style is perfect for the manner in which he perceives the attainment of freedom in America. That is, he moves in corporate structures; he moves in the financial world of Wall Street. Consequently, he has been forced to develop a different set of priorities; and these priorities (goals) must be consistent within his operating framework. It is impossible for Young to act like a Malcolm in that corporate framework. It is foolish to expect him to.

The present-day Negro leadership has no independent international position because it does not see the struggle in nationalist terms. And that is why it is dangerous. It is important not to fall into the trap of simply labeling these leaders as Uncle Toms. It is imperative that we have a clear understanding of the manner in which they view the world. This is the only way to fight them. They speak for thousands of Black people, and the failure of the militants to understand the reasons for that appeal would be disastrous. Psychologically, black America is conflicted about seeing itself as an integral part of American society. DuBois referred to this phenomenon as "double consciousness." This double consciousness has been implicit in the black man's history since the first slaves were brought here four hundred years ago. The struggle within the race has centered around the correct manner in which to destroy this double consciousness. Or in more precise political terms, it has been an internal struggle between the nationalists and the integrationists.

The integrationists do not believe that the basic socio-economic structure must be destroyed. But rather, that Negroes must simply be given a greater slice of the capitalistic action. They believe in reform not revolution. They are men who are essentially awed by the power of the Establishment. They have weighed the issues and decided that the best course lies in seeking some kind of rapprochement with the "system." The system is not bad at heart, they say, it just does not have enough black people in key jobs and fine houses.

Further, more in line with our topic, they believe that the struggle must be confined simply to giving Negroes rights as American citizens. Therefore, when King linked the struggle in Vietnam with the human rights struggle here in the United States, Wilkins, Young, and [Bayard] Rustin vehemently denounced him. They stated emphatically that not only was King's action tactically incorrect, but that there was no relationship between our struggle and the war in Vietnam. But it became clear in the months following Dr. King's remarks that the black man's relationship to that war is one of the key issues surrounding it. The rebellions in the cities further helped to illustrate the explicit relationship between the status of Afro-Americans and the war itself. While Whitney Young consistently made statements geared to assure the Johnson administration that the War on Poverty and the Vietnam War could be conducted with the same degree of intensity, there were rebellions in over fifty American cities. It became increasingly clear that the massive aid demanded in the cities and the massive resources necessary for waging war in Vietnam were at odds with each other.

Even though Young has never stated it, his trip last year to Vietnam for the apparent reason of speaking to Negro GIs strongly implies, in and of itself, that there is a functional relationship between those soldiers and the society to which they must return. And recently, almost ironically, we find Mr. Young a member of the unofficial fact-finding tour on the Vietnam elections. If Stokely Carmichael and King are wrong about the moral relationship of the war to black America, why did the president select a civil rights leader as a member of the fact-finding committee? Johnson was simply attempting to convince black people that they have a vital interest in the political and military conduct of the war. Further, he made a hypocrite of Young.

Thus, the established Negro leadership is forced to continue waging the fight for total liberation within the limits set by the oppressor. Or more precisely, it has constructed an ideology that naturally limits the contours of the struggle. This is a bad position for an oppressed minority to be in. It means that we are limited to alternatives imposed by a decadent government. It further means or assumes that the overall needs of black America can be fully satisfied within the framework of the American body politic. It assumes that the long-range interests of black America coincide with those of the white power structure.

The only way out of this trick-bag is to begin from the position that black people constitute a would-be nation apart from that of white America. Therefore, there are two Americas -a black one and a white one; and black America very clearly must decide its own destiny. It must independently decide what its interests are, both in the national and the international context. Consequently, it is no longer a question of civil rights for Negroes; but rather, it is a question of national liberation for black America. That means that we see ourselves as a "colonialized" people instead of as disenfranchised American citizens. That means that our struggle is one with the struggles of oppressed people everywhere, and we alone must decide what our stance will be toward those nations struggling to liberate themselves from colonial and neocolonial domination.

Currently, America is the chief neocolonialist power, exercising control over the resources of most of Africa and Latin America, while keeping the props under the politically stale regime of Thieu and Ky in Vietnam. The forces fighting for national liberation have had to increase the tempo of the struggle. But ultimately none of them can succeed as long as the United States remains the reactionary giant that it is. Finally the United States itself must have a total and complete revolution; and black America is the key to that revolution, and its potential vanguard. American foreign policy is essentially predicated on the maintenance of a stable society at home. But we are here, and the conditions under which we exist do not lend themselves to stability. We will have to struggle on every possible level to survive. And because of the nature of our historical experience, it is foolish to speak in terms of individual survival.

The civil rights movement spoke in terms of individual survival. Hence, it failed to understand the implicit nationalism of the masses of Black America. All of the nationalistic elements were there, but the Negro leadership refused to see or to acknowledge them. Therefore, when Whitney Young expresses a desire to discard the blues for Bach, or the "jitterbug" for the ballet, he is advocating the destruction of an identifiable Afro-American culture. He is advocating the destruction of the Black Nation. In European terms, the Negro leaders are intelligent men, but their failure to understand the revolutionary possibilities of black culture doomed the civil rights movement to oblivion.

Black Power is a natural response to the nationalist strivings of the masses of black America. It is implicitly based on the concept of nationhood. With this understanding, the attempts by Garvey, DuBois, Malcolm X, Robert Williams, and Stokely Carmichael to internationalize our struggle are dialectically consistent with the thrust of Afro-American history. For example, as a member of a national liberation front, Brother Stokely's recent trip to Havana, North Vietnam, Algeria, and the Middle East is perfectly logical. It connects the Afro-American nation to the larger context of the worldwide revolution; and at the same time, it breaks down the ideological walls which have contained the struggle thus far. It supplies the black theorist and activist with a new set of political alternatives. Like the guerrilla fighter, we have at our disposal the advantage of greater and more flexible tactical mobility. Only in this case the initial thrust of the movement is more political than military. It is important, therefore, that the political goals of the movement be expanded. The slogan Black Power should be more explicitly connected with the question of nationhood. The movement in the United States must become more consolidated; and national priorities must be advanced along with international priorities.

In order for this kind of strategy to bear fruit, the progressive wing of the Black Power movement must attack the narrowness that has plagued the struggle in recent years. This is within both camps, the nationalists' and the integrationists'.

We have already discussed the narrow ideology of the integrationists. But the nationalists have also displayed a limited view of the struggle. Here I refer specifically to the "back-to-Africa" advocates. Many of them have no revolutionary program, and therefore, see unity with Africa in purely racial terms. Consequently, there is a nationalist movement in Chicago now being organized to send thousands of people back to Liberia, which is itself in need of a revolution. Very few nationalists of this variety have ever analyzed the diversity of political systems in Africa. Very few of them have voiced a desire to join the liberation movements in Angola, Mozambique, and Zimbabwe (Southern Rhodesia). This latter is one of the most valid forms of support that we can offer our brothers and sisters in these regions.

The best course internationally is the linking together of all spheres of revolutionary activity in the Third World. This is the course recently taken by SNCC, RAM, and to a lesser degree by CORE. For example, SNCC sent delegates to the recent conference of Latin American revolutionaries and to key parts of Africa and Asia.

Wilkins's criticism of Carmichael's Havana trip deserves comment here. He attacked Stokely in what must be called essentially "nationalistic" terms, pointing out that the Havana trip betrayed the concept of an "all-black" movement. But SNCC has never claimed that a strictly all-black movement was consistently relevant in an international context. Theoretically, magazines like *Soulbook* and *Black America* had been saying this for quite some time. Wilkins betrays his reluctance to see the international ramifications of the black liberation movement when he writes:

> Now comes a public acknowledgment by spoken and written word, by picture and by physical presence that the "black" creation of these earnest young people is but a tail to another's kite. It is tied to Castro, to Chile and to South America, to Peking and to God knows what else. It is not a movement by black people for the improvement of black Americans here in America, but a movement whose direction depends upon people (not black) far from Rolling Fork, Miss., Terrell County, Ga., and the slums of Roxbury, Mass.

This does not prove, of course, that the Negro militants are Communists or that the drive of Negro Americans for their citizenship rights is communist. But the development sparked by Chief Black Power himself certainly suggests strongly that devotees of blackism may have been delivered into the orbit, if not into the actual hands, of non-blacks who are motivated by much more than singleminded dedication to the advancement of black people.

(*New York Post*, August 19, 1967)

It is clear that Wilkins's vision of freedom is radically different from Stokely's. The former envisions freedom in the simple context of American national life. The latter sees the contradiction between freedom in the United States and freedom gained at the expense of continued United States aggression abroad. Carmichael is aware of an implicit connection between a liberation movement in Terrell County and one in Angola and Chile. While Wilkins would make black America a party to white America's neocolonialist designs in Africa and Latin America, Carmichael is a revolutionary. Wilkins is a reformist. As such they see social and economic configurations quite differently.

Our choices must be separate ones. If it is important to have an independent black movement in this country which fights for the human rights of Black people, then that same movement must itself determine where it stands in the context of international affairs.

The movement is greatly in need of international allies. It must have what Maulana Karenga calls "functional unity." That is, it would seek a concrete coordination of political and military activities with the Third World. The first level of this functional unity would operate toward methods of destroying the psychology of colonialism. This level also involves a high degree of organization and communication between theorists and activists here and abroad. The political consciousness of black America must be broadened to give black people an understanding of its role in the destruction of oppression both here and abroad. Although military power is the foundation of the beast's power, we must understand the role of information and media as methods of controlling the oppressed. Internationally the United States Information Agency [USIA] determines how the Afro-American struggle will be seen. Black America must establish a unified information service in Africa, Asia, and Latin America. There can be no unity without communication.

The propaganda apparatus of the movement must become much more sophisticated than it is now. The recent Arab-Israeli war is a case in point. The Negro leadership voiced strong support of the Israelis during the conflict and they were given a great deal of exposure in the racist press. But the nationalists had no adequate means of presenting the Arab side of the conflict. So powerful was the pro-Israeli propaganda that most pro-Arab militants were labeled as racist "anti-Semites." Popular approval of Zionist aspirations in the Middle East is not based on Biblical mysticism, but on the cumulative results of good propaganda for over forty years.

An analysis of international realities clearly indicates that Zionist interests are decidedly pro-Western, and that these interests are neocolonialist in nature and design. In Africa, for example, a notable amount of the resources of the continent is controlled by Zionist-oriented Jews like the Rothschilds and Harry F. Oppenheimer whom Kwame Nkrumah calls "the king of mining in South Africa." It is the duty of the progressive elements of the movement to educate the community about these facts. Further, it is tactically dangerous to fall prey to emotional invective, and especially so on such matters as the Arab-Israeli conflict. Propaganda is most emotionally effective when it is precise, and based on facts that can be easily substantiated. The role of the revolutionary is to educate his people as he makes a revolution. And we cannot simply educate our people about domestic matters. Modern technology has made the factor of distances obsolete. There are no far-off places any more. Angola, Vietnam, and Chile are here, and we must deal with that reality in a manner that is understandable to the masses of black America.

Therefore, in the spirit of revolutionary concreteness, I put forth the following suggestions:

The U.S. War of Aggression in Vietnam. The attack against the Negro GIs who are fighting in the war should be better directed. The movement must not only criticize the "brothers' " involvement in that war, but it must offer meaningful alternatives. It must be first made clear to them that a national liberation army is needed at home. It should also be stressed that dignity for the black man cannot come at the expense of suppressing the legitimate aspirations of the Vietnamese people. We should advise these black soldiers to join the national liberation movements in Angola, Mozambique, and Zimbabwe (Southern Rhodesia). There they can fight the white colonialist honky. The war in Vietnam should be contrasted with the liberation struggles in Africa. Some of us should give up our American citizenship to fight in these places. In this way the unity that we seek is more functional than symbolic.

The United Nations. The question of the status of black America should be brought before the United Nations. Not because we have faith in that body, but for educational reasons. We should also attempt to maintain a permanent representative of black America at the United Nations. Contact between Afro-Americans and delegates to the UN must be broadened.

Liberation Front Offices. There should be liberation front offices (agencies) in all countries friendly to the cause of black liberation. These offices would counteract the activities of the CIA and the USIA. They could keep the lines of communication open between revolutionaries throughout the world. Their functions could be expanded as the situation worsens in America.

Cultural Exchange Programs. There should be cultural exchange programs between independent black institutions and the Third World. Black artists armed with the power of black culture should fan out all over the world spreading the soul message of black America. Recently, the CIA-controlled American Society for the Study of African Culture (AMSAC) participated in the Negro Arts Festival in Senegal, one of the most reactionary countries in Africa. Many Negro artists were thus exploited by the CIA by way of AMSAC. It is very important that the artistic community organize. Or it will find itself being manipulated in the propaganda war against the Third World. Black film makers should develop exchange programs. Films produced by black artists should be distributed all over the world. The same is true for tapes, photos, magazines, and revolutionary recordings.

All of these suggestions presuppose that Black Power is a revolutionary slogan. They also presuppose that strong independent organizations are now being developed in the black community. Without viable black organization here in the United States none of these things is possible. So the building of strong black institutions here in America must be the first consideration. These suggestions represent a tentative approach to the international implications of the Afro-American struggle. If the drift toward state-condoned fascism continues in the United States, many of these suggestions will have to be radically altered. We must be psychologically and physically prepared in the event that happens. But even a start in the direction outlined here will help develop the strength and resources necessary for liberation. The nature of what lies ahead is unknown. But the realities of the present give clear evidence that we must establish viable links with our brothers and sisters struggling in the Third World. We must develop revolutionary black institutions and be ready to defend them with our lives. We have no choices. All praise is due the Black Man.

Drama

INTRODUCTION

In Again, out Again, Larry Neal

Larry Neal. It was a winter evening in 1980. Cold. Larry Neal knocked on my front door at 2:30 in the morning. He was driving back to New York and stopped by in Philly to break and talk before attacking the icy turnpike through New Jersey. It had become a ritual, these unexpected, unannounced visits. We'd retire to my basement office, drink wine and talk the night away. I looked forward to them. Larry and I had been friends for thirty-five years and unexpected visits were things we both enjoyed. I remember this one because it was the last time he came to my home before his death in January of 1981. Came in shivering. Brown tweed jacket, leather cap, purple scarf around his neck.

"*Hawk* is in the wind, Cholly."

I put on a pair of dungarees, informed my suddenly awakened boys that it was just "Uncle Larry." The situation, familiar as it was, started them back to bed. They knew we were headed for the basement and another "private" talk.

"Goodnight, Uncle Larry."

My wife, Miriam, offered Larry something to eat. As always he would ask what she had cooked for dinner that night, and if he could make a sandwich out of that, he'd do so—if not, he'd ask for a sandwich with certain kinds of cold cuts and cheese. Once fortified with nourishment, we headed downstairs.

There is always gossip of a sort in the black literary community and after wading through that, Larry launched into a discussion of literature and our community because, as he said,

147

"We've forgotten how to use the language as a weapon, Cholly. See, Amiri and them already shot the arrow into the heart of American literature, and opened it in a way that it would be impossible to close blacks out of its bloodstream. But we need to do something else—take it a step further, because, Cholly!—we must find a way to overthrow the idea on this planet that whites are superior beings.

"Look at the images of us they're putting out there! And not just us! Africans! West Indians! The idea is that blacks are subservient to whites—that our humanity can only be realized in the service of whites!

"See, we've been dealing with the literature since the sixties in a kind of we-can-handle-English-too, and to a certain extent our parallel histories in America provide parallel opportunities to demonstrate areas where our similarities intersect. And the literature is one of them. I'm born in America, speak English, you're born in America, speak English also, there is bound to come a time when I will demonstrate that I can use English as well as you, we are, after all, launched from the same pad, on that level. And we've done a good job with that.

"Yet somehow, the literature hasn't made us collectively feel the equal of whites. So it has to liberate our feelings more— take pride in our beingness and drown that part of ourselves that fears self-realization. We have to see ourselves in another mode, seize our own reality and not flinch from the truth of it! Seize the history—retell it! Liberate it—from top to bottom— submit to rigorous challenge *everything* white folks have said about us. In some instances dismissing entire historical categories if we played a significant role in events and are not truthfully represented. Create an entirely new world view! *Blamm!* Like that!

"And not necessarily for the grand literary effect, or rewards in the white literary establishment. We *need* to dazzle black folks! Generate a desire for our tales in the bellies of our people. Find the right music to liberate our sensibilities, make black folks hungry for us—create lines outside black bookstores!

"Look at what the Jews have been able to do by exploiting their beingness in a hostile world. You don't even think of messing with Jews!

"We have to forge similar things in our own literature,

create it out of the fire, and hammer that mother while it's red hot—shape the idea of us *the way, we want it to be*—TURN THIS WORLD AROUND, Cholly! White folks don't give a damn about us because they don't believe they have to!

"We have to clean house—liberate the entire universe, Cholly, from the madness of white racism."

The conversation moved to other things. We had breakfast and Larry left around 10:00 that morning never having slept. I remember worrying, but it went that way with Larry sometimes. In again, out again, Larry Neal. I miss the visits, man.

—CHARLES FULLER

January 1989

From *The Glorious Monster in the Bell of the Horn* (1976)

The Glorious Monster in the Bell of the Horn was a three-act play produced by Woody King at the New York Federal Theater on July 6, 1979. This production was directed by Glenda Dickerson. This scene begins midway through Act 1.

(Spotlight scene)

DICKIE: Shammy, Shammy, you got to let me hide here for a few days . . . They're tracking me . . . I mean they're hunting me down.

SHAMMY: A few days?

DICKIE: Yes a few days . . .

SHAMMY: That's too long . . . Far too long.

DICKIE: A few hours then—

SHAMMY: That's worse . . .

DICKIE: What am I suppose to do then?

SHAMMY: You'll survive . . . You always do, but in the meantime I know something about the demons haunting you.

(DICKIE *paces back and forth, nervously puffing a cigarette. The sound of crackling laughter and mad screams are heard low in the background*)

DICKIE: You mean hunting me, don't you? I should have killed more of them . . .

SHAMMY: Who you talking about killing?

DICKIE: Them.

SHAMMY: Are they dead?

150

DICKIE: Decidedly so.

SHAMMY: And you? When are you dying? (SHAMMY *laughs*) Hunted . . . haunted . . . It's all the same thing . . . You're just part of a process . . . Like some cycle of pain . . . Yeah, like some awful thing that keeps recurring in my life, you dig, Davenport?

(Spotlight fades.

DICKIE *looks at* SHAMMY *in absolute contempt. Now they stare at each other.* DICKIE *breaks contact first.* SHAMMY *snaps his fingers. Suddenly there is literally a barrage of notes from Herbie's saxophone. The horn wails, screaming in some strange language. Both* DICKIE *and* SHAMMY *are momentarily stunned by the sound of the horn . . . but* DICKIE *is afraid. He snatches the 45 from his belt, but recovers quickly . . .* SHAMMY *laughs at* DICKIE *. . . The horn fades down in an elaborate cadenza. Music interlude. Blaring tune.*

Lights dim on DICKIE *and* SHAMMY *and come up on Herbie's ensemble)*

SHAMMY (continued): My monsters got to you, eh? That terror . . .

DICKIE: Monsters? Are they caged? Who the fuck is that anyway?

SHAMMY: Herbie Lee . . . Listen to that—

(The horn plays lower now, but restlessly, as if it were searching for something)

DICKIE: Herbie Lee, who?

SHAMMY: Hush! Just listen awhile.

(They listen as HERBIE *plays a line or two)*

SHAMMY (continued—whispers): Ain't he holy?

DICKIE (whispers): Herbie Lee, who?

SHAMMY (annoyed): Herbie Lee Robinson . . . Even though you're a fugitive, you must remember when his father used to play at the Blue Note on Ridge Avenue?

DICKIE: Yeah, we used to stand outside of the door 'cause they wouldn't let us in . . .

SHAMMY: We were too young, but they let Rose in though.

DICKIE: Ummmmh . . . Mr. Robinson got killed on the turn-
    pike going to New York . . . And . . . and his mother got
    killed too . . . It was a terrible accident . . .

SHAMMY: Yeah, it was terrible, but it wasn't so bad for Herbie.

DICKIE: What do you mean by that? Him losing his mother,
    and all the—

SHAMMY: It ain't a sad story . . . Herbie didn't lose nothing in
    that deal. Nothing at all . . . Even though he was only a
    baby when it happened at the time—

DICKIE: No . . . Shammy, he lost his mother . . . That . . .
    that was terrible in itself.

SHAMMY: Yes! It was terrible, a mean thing to happen . . . But
    you know what I heard?

DICKIE: No lies now, Shammy . . .

(Lights slowly rise on HERBERT ROBINSON, SR. *He has a
case with a saxophone in it. He calls to* VERA, *who is in the
wings)*

HERBERT: Come on baby, let's hit the road. We're running late.

VERA *(offstage)*: Just a minute, Herbert . . . I wanna see my
    little man, just one more time . . .

HERBERT: Make it fast, Randy is due any minute . . .

(Presently car horn blows)

HERBERT *(continued)*: That's him now . . . We got to hit the
    road, baby . . .

(VERA *enters wearing the purple dress and the flower in
her hair)*

VERA: You sure are in a hurry . . . Herbert . . . Sometimes all
    this rushing, this driving . . . I wish we could take little
    Herbie with us.

(The car horn blows again)

VERA *(continued)*: Damn that Randy! Can't he take it easy on
    that horn . . .

HERBERT: Herbie Lee's gonna be all right, baby, my brother
    Wallace is one of the best baby-sitters in North Philly . . .
    Come on let's get on the road . . . baby, and make that
    money . . .

(Silence. They listen to the music a moment. After several beats, SHAMMY *speaks)*

SHAMMY: Well anyway . . . They say when it happened Herbie's ole man was playing a tune. Some folks say it was a blues. But then again, it coulda been a jump tune. Coulda been any kind of tune . . . Yeah. Coulda been a ballad . . . Who knows? I wish I knew, really do. I suppose the only person who could know is Herbie Lee . . . But . . . sometimes . . . sometimes . . . I can see it like I was right there, in the car with them that night, right there, and the thick fog on the turnpike curling and foaming at us like ghosts . . . And, you see, Herbert's got his horn out now, polishing it . . . Taking care of it, like it was a baby ready for nursing . . . And then, he puts it in his mouth; and I am right there beside—it's winter, and we're wearing tweed suits, and I'm right there in the car, right there in the fog with the song . . . And Vera is wearing that purple dress, the one Wally bought her . . . Maybe that tune came from her first . . . I . . . I hadn't thought about that . . . Now . . . now Herbert, Mr. Robinson got that horn in his mouth . . . And . . . And, and, we don't see that broken down tractor-trailer in front of us . . . And we're laughing, and talking about Duke and Fletcher, and then . . . then Herbert starts playing this tune . . . This tune . . . This tune . . . Yeah, it was . . .

*(*SHAMMY *stops suddenly, almost exhausted. He takes a deep breath . . . He is panting now. He seems to be having difficulty breathing)*
DICKIE: You all right?

*(*SHAMMY *nods in the affirmative, but he stares into space as if he were in a trance)*
SHAMMY: Yeah . . . yeah . . . yeah . . . yeah, it was sudden. So sudden that Herbie's father didn't even have time, or didn't want to take that horn out of his mouth . . . And then . . . then the force of the collision drove the horn back and down his throat, yes, and the steel curled up and around them, and the horn, that horn, it pressed into his

head and body . . . And the state troopers came, they had to pry the horn out of his head . . . the battered instrument was splattered with blood, and bits of Herbert's guts clung to the keys . . .

(*Long pause . . . as* SHAMMY *brightens up*)
SHAMMY (*continued*): How you like that riff?

(*They both laugh*)
DICKIE: By the way, what happened to the horn?
SHAMMY: The what?
DICKIE: The horn.
SHAMMY: Oh, the horn . . . yeah. Some old black man over on Taylor Street fixed it.
DICKIE: Well, how could he? . . . since you just said it was—
SHAMMY: It was smashed up all right; but this ole man is like a tinker, you know . . . Fucks around with all kinds of gadgets and do . . . *They* say that after the funeral Wally Robinson, Herbert's brother, was approached by this ole guy who said he could fix it . . .
DICKIE: And did he fix it?
SHAMMY: Yes, he did . . . he fucked around with it until it was almost new . . . and gave it to Herbie Lee . . .
DICKIE: My God . . . No wonder . . . He sounds so . . .
SHAMMY: Frightening?
DICKIE: Weird . . .
SHAMMY: Weird? A weird word, "weird." Maybe some lost language, eh Davenport? Had you ever thought about that, college boy . . . Doctor . . . Doctor? Yeah, weird, weird all right like some glorious monster bursting free . . . This is gonna be a complicated evening, Davenport . . . My magic—
DICKIE: Well let me out of this then . . .
SHAMMY: I can't . . . We're into my show now.
DICKIE: Too far where?
SHAMMY: Into it. Too far into the maw of madness . . .
DICKIE: I've changed my mind about you writing the wedding skit . . . I can now make other arrangements.
SHAMMY: Punk. Other arrangements? A dead man making other arrangements?

DICKIE: There's still time before the wedding—

SHAMMY: (*almost shouting*): Time?! You don't know what time is, fool! Think of that time, and this time, we call now . . . This time which is not, and which is; you are that time, and this time, tonight, the captain, and your father, the good doctor, will—

(SHAMMY *stops talking . . . We can softly hear a* WOMAN *humming the blues . . . The voice sounds off in the distance . . . Now we can also faintly hear the wail of a train whistle cutting the August night . . . Presently,* MADAME BLUE *slowly dances across the stage. She wears a blue transparent veil; she is naked underneath the veil . . . She dances with a staff which is shaped like a serpent . . . She dances across the stage to a place upstage where there is a scrim of gossamer texture. Behind the scrim, there is a bed that represents her sanctuary.* DICKIE *stares at the* WOMAN, *and then turns to* SHAMMY *who looks at the* WOMAN *with* DICKIE . . . *Neither of them acknowledges her presence, although it is clear that they have both seen her . . . And now* DICKIE *slowly pulls out the Army 45.* SHAMMY *starts dancing a kind of jitterbug soft-shoe . . .* SHAMMY *dances intermittently throughout the following sequence . . . Now* DICKIE *examines the weapon carefully*)

SHAMMY (*continued*): You know, Davenport? I have discovered madness . . .

DICKIE: And how the hell does one discover madness?

(SHAMMY *does a quick dance*)

SHAMMY: I did . . . I did . . . I did . . . but this . . . but this . . . this madness is lucid . . . (*Dance*) rational. (*Dance*) And it has shape like that forty-five in your hand. (*Dance*)

(DICKIE *now points the gun at* SHAMMY)

DICKIE: Madness, rational? You have a strange way with words—

(SHAMMY *continues to dance*)

SHAMMY YEAH! Sometimes, you should know about it . . . You're mad too.

DICKIE: But mad and madness are different entities, ole buddy . . .

SHAMMY: Well look at the college boy, talking smart for once in his life . . .

DICKIE: All you low-class-crabs-in-the-barrel niggers hate me, don't you?

SHAMMY: You could call it that.

DICKIE: Well then, it's time to turn this set around . . . (*He engages the gun*) I'm tired of you fucking with me, Shammy . . . (*He gestures with the gun*) Now go on tell me more about your discovery of madness . . . Was that woman part of it? Or is she just another one of your pretenses, your shadows, your illusions?

SHAMMY: Now that prop is madness, not my astrological criss-cross . . . Not my pretense, my illusions, my pretext, but that precision you hold in your hands, doctor . . . It has nice weight . . . It's just a perfect little killing machine— Forty-five caliber . . .

DICKIE: I know that.

SHAMMY: I'm sure you do.

DICKIE: (*wilder*): Stop fucking around!!! Go on and beg for your life, nigger!

SHAMMY: Easy, soldierboy . . . Easy . . . It weighs about four pounds . . .

DICKIE: Every real GI knows that jody-jody . . .

(*Now they begin to circle each other . . . DICKIE points the gun at SHAMMY still*)

SHAMMY: The model number is nineteen-dash-eleven-dash-A-one.

(*Dance*)

SHAMMY (*continued*): The muzzle velocity is eight-hundred and two feet per second . . . The white man developed it to fight the Moros in the Philippines . . . Shoot me!!! The shell weighs two-hundred and thirty grams . . . And it's copper clad . . . Can't you see how illogical it all is? How this madness is so illogical as to be rational . . . Shooooot me motherfucker!!!!

DICKIE: You're going in circles, Shammy . . .

(The lights start dimming . . . SHAMMY *is dancing slowly away from* DICKIE *. . .* SHAMMY *dances into the darkness, spotlight comes up on* DICKIE *as the rest of the stage darkens)*

SHAMMY *(in the dark):* Yes, mad like you, locked inside the magician's curlicuing patterns of dead ash and memory . . .

(Echo in house)

DICKIE: Don't leave me alone like this! Shammy! Shammy! Shammy!

(There is a drum solo as DICKIE *fires the gun into the darkness. We can hear* SHAMMY *laughing between the gun bursts.* DICKIE *fires and the horn screams in the night. Applause from the tables.*

The lights come up slowly on the barber's chair, and a small cabinet behind it. There is a radio on the cabinet. The spotlight holds on the chair throughout the following radio announcement. First, we hear snatches of Charlie Parker's "Now's the Time":)

RADIO ANNOUNCER (RAVIN' RAYMOND): Dateline: Somewhere in the Pacific . . . It was disclosed today that colored troops have been active in a major military offensive against Japanese troops . . . All Negro units led by Colonel Wilmer F. Lucas have destroyed key Japanese defensive bunkers and are now in the mopping-up stages of what has been a grueling battle . . . Walter White, Secretary of the N double A.C.P. says that the recent wave of Negro victories in the war against fascism puts a lie to the myth that the Negro soldier is incapable of sustained military combat . . . And he further—

*(*WALLY ROBINSON, *a pouchy man with deep brown skin, in his early fifties, enters and snaps off the radio. He looks around at the posters hanging above the stage, especially the banner reading: "Support Our Tan Tanks." He nods in the affirmative . . . Now he primps in an imaginary mirror while singing, "Vootney on the Vautney." Next, he picks up a* Philadelphia Tribune *. . . There is a large headline about Marian Anderson on it . . . He sits down in*

the chair and begins to read the paper . . . We can hear
HERBIE LEE *intermittently practicing his scales*)

WALLY (*to the audience and patrons at the cafe tables*): You
know, this barbershop used to be the best place to come
and sit and think, but lately—Well anyway I'm glad you
stopped by . . . I . . . I . . . have to tell you my side of
this warped tale before we all go mad . . . Yes, my friends,
mad like Shammy with this twisted act he wants to lay on
us . . . But I know all of this scheming and dreaming
started when Rose—

(*He is interrupted by the entry of two of Iverson's* DISCIPLES.
They whisper something to WALLY *and leave. Presently*
PETER IVERSON *enters surrounded by two* DISCIPLES.
IVERSON *is carrying a cane in one hand, and a large book
in the other . . . There is a haughty air about him . . . He
uses the cane like a swagger stick . . . He wears dark,
formal clothing which gestures in the direction of aristocratic taste. He wears a black bowler hat. There is something sinister in this elegance; but there is a softness about
his eyes . . . He takes off the hat slowly, and hands it to
one of his* DISCIPLES—*He seems very anxious to serve
him.* WALLY *gets out of the chair, and brushes it off for*
IVERSON. IVERSON *eases into the chair talking*)

IVERSON: I have an important appointment today, Wallace . . .
Let us say an appointment with destiny . . . "Destiny"
—is that too literary for this occasion, Wallace? (*He laughs*)
You should learn to understand the idea of destiny, Wallace . . . Yes, consider it: "Appointment with Destiny."

(*Long pause . . .* HERBIE *plays another scale . . . Then
stops abruptly . . . Long pause again . . . The sound of
clippers*)

IVERSON (*continued*): Yes, destiny . . . It's a good word, Wallace . . . The destiny of the colored peoples of the world . . .

WALLY: Henson says you lost your job at the arsenal . . .

IVERSON: Of course the arsenal . . . Chief technician in
charge of maintenance—

WALLY: Henson says they fired you as a security risk, and he—

IVERSON: Security risk? That's a laugh . . . In their system, any
    intelligent colored man is a security risk . . . But Henson
    is confused . . .
WALLY: How?
IVERSON: Because, I terminated my position of my own
    accord . . .
WALLY: I see, but that's the word on the avenue—
IVERSON: Henson is spreading ignorance . . . But then again,
    perhaps that is his function, his work in life, just as my
    role is to bring light . . . Henson and Negroes like him
    have never been able to get the facts straight . . . Never!
    And that's what's wrong with the race, Wallace . . . Her
    children are fighting a war, and they don't begin to know
    who the real enemy is . . . It's all confusion . . . But . . .
    but they'll know soon . . .
WALLY: Turn this way just a minute. (*There is a long pause
    while* WALLY *concentrates on the trimming*) . . . Speaking
    about the war—
IVERSON (*musing*): If they could only get the facts straight . . .
    The facts. We have so much to do . . . What was that you
    said?
WALLY: I was gonna ask what you thought Truman's next move
    was gonna be? They say this war is almost over . . .
IVERSON: That's a lie! This government is lying . . . This war
    won't end until—
WALLY: Damn, Pete! How would *you* know they're lying?
IVERSON: Because they *always* lie. They can't help but lie. It is
    their nature to lie. That's why this war . . . this war will
    continue . . . They have lied about so many things: sci-
    ence, art, history—
WALLY: Henson said that *they* suspected you of being a secu-
    rity risk . . . Pro-Jap, he called you—

(IVERSON *starts to respond, but they are interrupted by*
HERBIE LEE *who slowly walks across the stage playing his
saxophone. He walks to barber's chair where* WALLY *stands.
He stops playing the song momentarily as he motions for
Wally's attention.* WALLY *leans closer as* HERBIE *makes
some speechlike sounds on the horn.* WALLY *nods as if he
understands what* HERBIE *is saying on the horn. Then*

HERBIE *starts playing again as he nods goodbye to* WALLY *and* IVERSON. WALLY *goes back to the barber's chair. He and* IVERSON *continue their conversation in pantomime . . .*

HERBIE LEE *walks out of the circle of light around the chair. The light fades down on the chair, and comes up slowly on the gazebo where* ROSE *is writing something in a red notebook. Birds chirp, leaves rustle softly.* ROSE *does not see* HERBIE *. . . She begins reading aloud from the manuscript . . . She is reciting the poem that she has just written . . . After several beats* HERBIE *accompanies her with the horn)*

ROSE:
That red flowering August
I wanted to grasp my own sun
and sing my own song . . .

(*She pauses a little to correct something on the page . . . She looks up as* HERBIE *plays a line . . . He motions for her to continue*)

You see
It would be my song
flaming there . . .
the feel of you alive in me
all tar and planet swirling
in this womb
I offer you lover . . .

In this body
which is our body
and the sun's body
which is God's body . . .

I feel your flame
between these hot thighs
this body
is holy
is a place of truth . . .

(*Now they embrace. The light goes back around them and then slowly fades up on the barbershop. Back in the shop another* MAN *has joined the group. His name is* CHRIS HENSON. *He is dressed in a white shirt with a civil defense band around the sleeves . . . He also wears a civil defense helmet. A whistle hangs from a string around his neck. He is fiercely patriotic . . .* HENSON *looks the* DISCIPLES *of* IVERSON *over and then glances quickly at* IVERSON. *Their eyes meet . . . They both break contact about the same time.* WALLY *is brushing* IVERSON *off*)

WALLY: So you knew Marcus Garvey, eh?

IVERSON: Yes, I knew the man . . . Well, what can we say? He was the new light—

WALLY: I always wonder why they gave him such a hard time . . .

(IVERSON *is standing now, as he prepares to leave . . . He looks hard at* WALLY *now*)

IVERSON: You know what amazes and amuses me, Wallace?

WALLY: What?

IVERSON: That a man as intelligent as you should be so ignorant of the facts . . . Don't you realize that Garvey was building a *Black* army? Didn't you know that?

(IVERSON *inspects himself in the imaginary mirror as he pulls his wallet out . . . After a long pause*)

WALLY: Well no . . . I didn't know about that—

IVERSON (*to the* DISCIPLES): This is our problem, my brothers . . . (*To* WALLY): Yes an all-colored army, staffed with all-colored personnel from top to bottom . . . If he had lived we would be well on our way to taking Africa by now—

WALLY: Taking it? From whom?

IVERSON: From the beast, of course.

WALLY: The what?

IVERSON: Yes, the beast . . . That is how we designate the European . . . (*There is another pause while* IVERSON *looks himself over in the imaginary mirror again; the mirror hangs in front of the audience*)

HENSON (*quietly and firmly*): It all sounds like a Jap conspiracy to me . . . Black Nazis . . .

(EVERYONE *slowly gives his attention to* HENSON. *But*
IVERSON *continues to ignore* HENSON *as he checks himself
out in the mirror. He puts the hat on, ever so carefully
and blocks it. When he speaks, he addresses his men
instead of* HENSON)

IVERSON: Now you see what I have been talking about?
Now you understand why we grieve over the fate of our
people . . .

(*They nod in agreement*)

IVERSON (*continued*): This is the ignorance that we must triumph
over, my brothers . . .

HENSON: Ignorance . . . Shit . . . Why is it that all the nigger
intellectuals who talk like you are for those goddamn Japs!?

WALLY: Let it go, Chris!

HENSON: No! I can speak . . . He's always coming around here
talking that mess about the "colored peoples of the world."

(*Iverson's* DISCIPLES *are very agitated by this remark*)

IVERSON: These are the facts both real and metaphysical. It is
time to confront that chaos which is our role and design.
We know we were made to rule.

HENSON: You'll never rule me—

IVERSON: He would rather be ruled by the beast, by the slime
. . . I would say that his condition is somewhat, tragic . . .

(IVERSON *and his* MEN *laugh*)

HENSON: That monkey-chaser was a swindler just like you . . .
A damn charlatan, if there ever was one. He beat my
stupid brother out of a lot of money . . . You talking about
the facts . . . You're against God, this country . . . And
you hate us, Iverson . . . You hate us all!!! And that's why
I have vowed to crush you and your evil schemes!

(HENSON *jumps to his feet*)

WALLY: Cool it Chris! . . . It's nothing . . .

IVERSON (*to his* DISCIPLES): Sit him down . . .

(*They move toward* HENSON)

HENSON: Don't touch me.

(They begin to approach HENSON . . . WALLY *picks up his razor)*

WALLY: Okay, okay, everybody be cool . . . I pays the mortgage here . . .

IVERSON: Well then, tell him to sit down and learn something.

WALLY: When are you both gonna get tired of this? It's been going on for years . . .

IVERSON: It's taking that long to teach him . . .

WALLY: Come on Pete, say your piece . . . So this place can get back to normal . . .

HENSON: Why should he always have the last word? This is a free country . . .

(IVERSON *and his* DISCIPLES *laugh)*

IVERSON: Fool, you have no country, Mr. Henson. Don't you understand that? And in the coming whirlwind, we will destroy you, and make your memory obsolete . . . I don't think there is any need to tarry here any longer . . . Do you?

(They exit. IVERSON *is laughing as the lights fade down on the barbershop.*

A spotlight comes up on SHAMMY, *who is putting on a white beard and a straw hat. He has a corncob pipe in his mouth. He walks downstage and looks around. He walks with a distinct limp like an old man. He carries a gnarled cane. When he speaks his voice has the slight feeling of a Southern black preacher)*

SHAMMY: Them bones . . . Them talking bones chillen . . . Yes . . . Yes . . . chillen . . . In the ole days they used to carry the slaves out into the woods when they killed them . . . Yes chillen . . . when they killed them . . . They . . . They . . . jest leave em there just like animals . . . They didn't even bury em then . . . The bodies would just lay out under the sun for the buzzards to gnaw on . . . Well, my chillen . . . One day this ole slave name John was walkin' through the woods; and he sees this, this here skeleton . . . laying there in the sun . . . He don't pay them dry bones no mind . . . cause he done see plenty of them bones in his time . . . Well don't you know chillen, he sits down on that rock to rest his weary self; and the next thing you know, he hears somebody eerie say: "Tongue is the cause of my being here." Well, don't you know! John jumped up, and looked around, and he didn't see nobody, but the skeleton . . . "What's that you say?" John asked to no one in particular . . . And then he heard the skull say spooky like: "Tongue is the cause of my being here." John leaped up and ran back to the Master . . . "Massa . . . Massa . . ." he say, "there's a talking skeleton in the woods!" Old master say, "I don't believe that John, you're not trying to make a fool of me are you?" John say: "No Massa, dem bones is *really* talking." So the Master called all of his friends from all of the nearby plantations . . . White folks came from all over; and when they arrived at the place of the skeleton—the place of the talking bones—they said to John: "Make him speak." But the skeleton wouldn't talk . . . So, and then, they beat John to death with anything that they could get their hands on . . . And left him beside the other skeleton . . . And as the sun set redly, the buzzards was tearing into John's liver, and as the waning sun shined through his vacant sockets . . . the bones laying beside him commenced to shake and rattle, and then, chillen, them bones spoke . . . They said: "Tongue, yes tongue brought *us* here, and tongue brought *you* here too . . ."

(SHAMMY *waves the cane, and points it in the direction of Doctor Davenport's office . . . The light comes up on the office as* SHAMMY *limps offstage tapping the cane and singing an old field song*)
PUBLIC ADDRESS SYSTEM (*a very nasal female voice*): Doctor Davenport . . . Doctor Davenport . . . Pick up on five-two please . . . Doctor Davenport . . . Doctor Davenport, on five-two please . . .

(DOCTOR DAVENPORT *is dressed in a white medical smock. His scope hangs around his neck . . . He holds an X-ray photo up to the light . . . He makes a notation in his log . . . The telephone rings now almost incessantly . . . He*

*can hardly finish entering the notes. Exasperated, he picks
up the phone)*

DAVENPORT (*on the phone*): What?! The emergency room?
Who's available now? . . . Have you tried to reach Doctor
Redman . . . ? What about Klein? He's good with those
kind of cases . . . He's in surgery now? I see . . . I'll be
there as soon as possible . . . Is Doctor Fuller on the
floor? Yes Fuller!!! That new intern from Howard . . .
Well send him down there . . . I'll be along shortly . . .

*(He begins working on his notebook again . . . He seems
to be writing faster now. The phone rings again. He
tries to ignore it, but he can't . . . He snatches up the
phone)*

What is it this time Maggie! (*Long pause as a strange look
comes over Davenport's face*) The what? The what? Military police? Well . . . what—

(Right at this moment a short black MAN *dressed in a
captain's uniform enters the doctor's office . . . He wears
an armband which indicates that he is an MP. He is
flanked by two very tall Negro MPs.* CAPTAIN DABNEY *is
smoking a large cigar. He looks around Davenport's office
with approval. When he speaks, he will have a deep Southern accent.* DOCTOR DAVENPORT *is still holding the phone
dumbfounded. The two MPs are armed, and they stand at
the ready)*

CAPTAIN DABNEY: You are Doctor Richard Davenport, Senior,
suh?

*(DAVENPORT nods his head slowly in the affirmative, as he
hangs up the phone)*

CAPTAIN DABNEY (*continued—in a spiel*): Captain Dabney here,
suh! Yes, suh! Capn Dabney, here under the order of the
President of these United States as executed through the
direct command of General B. Wright Carter, suh! We are
conducting a legal search of these premises under section
five-sixty-one, article number seven of the uniform articles
of woe, suh!

(Now DOCTOR DAVENPORT *moves from behind the desk.*
There is something ridiculous and insane about DABNEY)

DAVENPORT: My God man, what is this all about?

DABNEY: You are Doctor Davenport, suh?

DAVENPORT: Yes, but—

DABNEY: The father of PFC Richard B. Davenport, Junior,
suh?

DAVENPORT: Yes sir, but where, what?

DABNEY: And—

DAVENPORT: What has Richard done?

DABNEY: And said Richard B. Davenport, Junior, suh, resides
at your residence in the twenty-four hundred block of
North Twenty-fifth Street . . . Is that right, suh?

DAVENPORT: Of course, Richard lives there!!!

DABNEY: Therefore, under section six-seventy-nine, article eighty-
five, and chapter twenty-two, I am empowered under the
military laws of these United States and the President to
arrest your son and bring him before the military tribunal
in Jefferson County—

DAVENPORT: Speak clearly, fool! What has my son done?

DABNEY: Under the aforementioned sections, and with specific
reference to section seven-twelve, article one-eighteen,
chapter twenty-two, PFC Davenport is charged with the
following military crimes: Illegally procuring weapons . . .

DAVENPORT: Oh my God!

DABNEY: . . . and the assault therewith; desertion, section
six-seventy-nine, article eighty-five; and murder . . .

DAVENPORT: Murder? Not my Richard . . .

DABNEY: Yes, murder, section seven-twelve, articles one-eighteen
to seven-thirteen—an article one-nineteen, suh!!!

(DABNEY *snaps his heels*)

DAVENPORT: Richard Davenport? There must be some kind of
mistake . . .

(Now DOCTOR DAVENPORT *just numbly stands there look-*
ing at DABNEY . . . *Then he slumps slowly down in the*
chair as he looks vacantly into space . . . The lights start
their slow and inevitable fade)

DABNEY: It's no mistake, Doctor.

(BARON SATURDAY *enters awesome and drunk, blowing a whistle madly as he does his death-dance. Meanwhile the* PUBLIC ADDRESS SYSTEM:)

PUBLIC ADDRESS SYSTEM: Doctor Davenport . . . Doctor Davenport . . . Doctor Davenport . . . Doctor Davenport . . . Doctor DavenportDavenportDavenport . . .

(DABNEY *lights his cigar as the lights go out*)

Poetry

INTRODUCTION

Larry's Time

It's good to have the opportunity to take a closer look at the poetry of Larry Neal. Great to see the porkpie hat, the pegged legged boys with polished saxophones, the ears flying into space, distant orishas, the sun sperms exploding and hear the thick thudding sounds and the juju wonder songs of his world again. Larry Neal jumped into the middle of the whirlpool of cultural activity in the early 1960s and 70s. A young man. A young poet/writer/activist, with friends and associates who together doo wopped, finger popped, name dropped, orally bounced information off of each other, offered social and political comments to audiences, and produced books, magazines and articles that gave voice to unheard voices of alternative attitudes and viewpoints. Larry Neal, smack dab in the center of the swirl of events, teaching, writing, linking his poetry to the black struggle for liberation, stood in the front row of the literary part of the march for civil rights, the literary part of the need for revolution. He wrote about Malcolm X, Frantz Fanon, the Watts & Newark rebellions, historical African roots, and the current affairs affecting people in his community. Neal, an urban poet, syncopating and mixing dissonant levels of insults, mythologies, ideologies, appropriations, clichés and rhetoric as poetic combinations, was still evolving, still in the first draft of his research when "touched by death's whisper." Now we can examine some of the aspects of his poetic experience.

—JAYNE CORTEZ

January 30, 1989

The Narrative of the Black Magicians

For Ahada

Fast fly the faces through our blood years,
faces fly by the widows of the moon
and pass the sons of the slaves kneeling
on the shores of home.
time in their faces stops. and the dance
is stilled by the chained sea whose sounds
bring in memories out of our private and collective past.

The sea contains our dreams, tight, pressed;
contains conversation under the ship's
floor prisons:
touchless hands, I lay beside you,
lips part in fever,
and the receding drums
telling of a new death.

Great Shango help us . . .

Faces peer up into the rocking darkness:
this is the ocean that birthed us newly;
but the chained sea is hostile,
white madnesses lurk in children's dreams.

O Jordan roll on to no end . . .

These faces live to appear on the land that became
theirs by their blood,
made ours by our blood.

172

These faces appear in swampy places bundled
in motherless callings,
appear on the slave blocks, sold into fear
sold to a sunless, drumless people.

Their appearances flicker above the plotting fires—
they plan night death to pale monsters.
faces mute. the fire burns visions
into his eyes. in his hands blood burns.

Eastward their faces turn, moving eyes strain
for the horizon.
these faces slither under cabinet doors and see
themselves in strange cities.
they mouth that language awkwardly in an eastern
bluesness . . .
Faces under the timeless sky. their sky.
made by them. made for them.

These faces catch Scottsboro freight North,
sing blues for the river gods,
turn up weird in Memphis, Dallas, Chicago,
Kansas City . . .
hammered steel out of those mountains;
laid their lives down in spite of themselves
as steel killed them in narrow tunnels.

They laughed with John Henry
and played spy with Harriet Tubman
and strong ones mostly.
These faces pour out of slavetime
in the subways of fear,
jockey for life between gray crushing mountains
and the 42nd Street movies . . .
See these faces . . . they saw their best
killed in bleak winters, and their homes
upheaved by the progress blood-drinking machines . . .

Faces that flew past the president's coffin,
who saw their leaders busy at moaning
betrayals. who, in spite, managed to love.

Child faces, blackly playing on those back streets
are children of gods and the Lion.
faces charged with change; these faces turn
from the west, turn inward eyes on themselves,
address the black cosmos, are gods.
dancing faces making this Earth breathe
in green blackness.

Our bones are in this land.

It must be ours in the living.

O Ancestor faces form on film our minds
form our contours out of deep wailing saxes.
form in the voice our would-be leaders.
form child. form in the rush of war.
form child. form in the sun's explosion
and in the avenging waves.
form in the prisons of America.
form child. form your image of men
and women tearing into the open;
and face the form of our love in the final
clasping and embrace;
form your face out of the Earth;
form your face with searing waves of sound,
as beyond the wall there is a painful calm . . .

1965/70

Shine's Sermon on Cosmology I

Screaming deep down jungle hot and seamy when the world
was word and kinda dreamy. Who that, the who that, screaming when down hot screams of careening shadows. Shine seems
as light against deep deep low moaning song of mumbling

mammy magic. Who him care there? He exhorts: Give me your shoes from Florsheims and your vines from Lester's, and I will lead you into the who what where of ever ecstasy. Yea, and my Lord will smite them those haggard bullshitting singers of ass reaming straight talk. Stretch forth your jungle world hands and plunge them between starry thighs. Hey now. Are you ready for this? Whose ghosts walks there? Is him the hoodoo freedom, or the metaphor of the machine gun metaphysicians. Go on kiss the man, Sister. He won't bite you. He'll just ram coke bottles up your pussy . . . But dig: low grumbling light comes with reeling specters of bebop wisdom. Hating order. Hating history. Sullen bitch, pummeling gods in the ever ecstasy of the when how. Where now is the who where? Sock 'em constellations, worlds of words that lie. Shine be him who comes in the where when how of honky-tonk murders. Words smash against tiger suits. Slam of forty-four against box-coat stride pianists, and flap-jack comedians. Who you think, so what you are not . . .

Shine Goes to Jail

There was no toilet to speak of. And they gave us old newspapers to wipe our asses with. There was only this rut running through the cell. It was flushed three times a day with water from a special pump. The water was mixed with pine oil disinfectant. There is this cell. It's supposed to accommodate three men, but there are four of us here right now. Woody Neal from Georgia, down around Atlanta; Silas T. Washington, over here, he's near Titusville, Alabama; I know his folks. Blind Jack, sitting there yonder with his guitar; well he from Florence, Tennessee, same as Handy. And me? I'm from everywhere . . .

Shine Touched by Death's Whisper

Gray trees and the song
O how we murder our sinews
the bodies wronged by looming fear
the grim fantastic knife
cutting the humid air and his throat.

See how the jagged toothed murderer
dances on the edge of his glass?

I Shine say there is a putrid wind
blowing through those sockets
I say we bear the death din
as well as the cooing song
of the lovers among the summer grasses.

a demon memory this is
those specters, those echoes
those persistent ancestor warnings
and the magic   and the magic we
know we have lost   and strive to retain

O Singer!!!

1974

Poppa Stoppa Speaks from His Grave

Remember me baby in my best light,
lovely hip style and all;
all laid out in my green velour
stashing on corners
in my boxcar coat—
so sure of myself, too cool for words,
and running down a beautiful game.

It would be super righteous
if you would think of me that way sometimes;
and since it can't be that way,
just the thought of you digging on me that way
would be hip and lovely even from here.

Yeah, you got a sweet body, baby,
but out this way, I won't be needing it;
but remember me and think of me
that way sometimes.

But don't make it no big thing though;
don't jump jive and blow your real romance.
but in a word, while you high-steppin and finger-poppin
tell your lovin' man that I was a bad
motherfucker till the Butcher cut me down.

1969

Don't Say Goodbye to the Porkpie Hat

Mingus, Bird, Prez, Langston, and them

Don't say goodbye to the Porkpie Hat that rolled
along on nodded shoulders
                     that swang bebop phrases
                     in Minton's jelly roll dreams
Don't say goodbye to hip hats tilted in the style of a soulful era;
the Porkpie Hat that Lester dug
swirling in the sound of sax blown suns
                     phrase on phrase, repeating bluely
                     tripping in and under crashing
                     hi-hat cymbals, a fickle girl
                     getting sassy on the rhythms.
Musicians heavy with memories
move in and out of this gloom;
the Porkpie Hat reigns supreme
smell of collard greens
and cotton madness
commingled in the nigger elegance of the style.
                     The Porkpie Hat sees tonal memories
                     of salt peanuts and hot house birds
                     the Porkpie Hat sees . . .
Cross riffing square kingdoms, riding midnight Scottsboro
trains. We are haunted by the lynched limbs.
On the road:
It would be some hoodoo town
It would be some cracker place
you might meet redneck lynchers
face to face
but mostly you meet mean horn blowers
running obscene riffs
Jelly Roll spoke of such places:
the man with the mojo hand

the dyke with the .38
the yaller girls
and the knifings.

Stop-time Buddy and Creole Sydney
wailed in here. Stop time.
chorus repeats, stop and shuffle.
stop and stomp.
listen to the horns, ain't they mean?
now ain't they mean
in blue
in blue
in blue streaks of mellow wisdom
blue notes
coiling around
the Porkpie Hat
and ghosts of dead musicians drifting through
here on riffs that smack
of one-leg trumpet players
and daddy glory piano ticklers
who
twisted arpeggios
with diamond-flashed fingers.
There was Jelly Roll Morton, the sweet mackdaddy,
hollering Waller, and Willie The Lion Smith—
some mean showstoppers.

Ghosts of dead holy rollers ricocheted in the air funky
with white lightnin' and sweat.
Emerald bitches shot shit in a kitchen smelling
of funerals and fried chicken.
Each city had a different sound:
there was Mambo, Rheba, Jeanne;
holy the voice of these righteous sisters.

Shape to shape, horn to horn
the Porkpie Hat resurrected himself
night to night, from note to note
skimming the horizons, flashing bluegreenyellow lights
and blowing black stars

and weird looneymoon changes; chords coiled about him
and he was flying
fast
zipping
past
sound
into cosmic silences.
And yes
and caresses flowed from the voice in the horn in the blue
of the yellow whiskey room where bad hustlers with big
coats moved, digging the fly sister, fingerpopping while
tearing at chicken and waffles.

The Porkpie Hat loomed specter like, a vision for the world;
shiny, the knob toe shoes,
sporting hip camel coats
and righteous pin stripes—
pants pressed razor shape;
and caressing his horn, baby like.

So we pick up our axes and prepare
to blast the white dream;
we pick up our axes
re-create ourselves and the universe,
sounds splintering the deepest regions
of spiritual space
crisp and moaning voices
leaping in the horns of destruction,
blowing death and doom to all who have no use for the spirit.

So we cook out of sight
into cascading motions of joy delight
shooflies the Bird lollygagging
and laughing for days,
and the rhythms way up in there
wailing, sending scarlet rays, luminescent,
spattering bone and lie.
we go on cool lords
wailing on into star nights,
rocking whole worlds, unfurling song on song

into long stretches of green spectral shimmerings,
blasting on, fucking the moon with the blunt edge
of a lover's tune, out there now, joy riffing
for days and do
railriding and do
talking some lovely shit and do
to the Blues God who blesses us.

No, don't say goodbye to the Porkpie Hat—
he lives, oh yes.

Lester lives and leaps
Delancey's dilemma is over
Bird lives
Lady lives
Eric stands next to me
while I finger the Afro-horn
Bird lives
Lady lives
Lester leaps in every night
Tad's delight
is mine now
Dinah knows
Richie knows
that Bud is Buddha
that Jelly Roll dug juju
and Lester lives
in Ornette's leapings
the Blues God lives
we live
live
spirit lives
and sound lives
bluebird lives
lives and leaps
dig the mellow voices
did the Porkpie Hat
dig the spirit in Sun Ra's sound
dig the cosmic Trane
dig be

dig be
dig be
spirit lives in sound
dig be
sound lives in spirit
dig be
yeah ! ! !

spirit lives
spirit lives
spirit lives
SPIRIT ! ! !

SWHEEEEEEEEEEEEEEETTT ! ! !

take it again
this time from the top

The Slave

For LeRoi Jones

Along the streets
        the stores are barricaded,
black upheaval,
        what moves is ours.
death counts their dead
        wall street is burning
nbc (nigger broadcasting co.)
        plays muddy waters and mahalia
for a black army shitting destruction
        upon gomorrah falling

Orpheus black king-pin singing blues
        out of an M-1.

take what is left
        build brightly colored huts
and dance with the children,
        clear the air good
their ashes would even contaminate
        confusing our rhythms
now we are slaves for ourselves.

The Baroness and the Black Musician

Tangled in sea weed minutes;
her eyes suck your blood.
the baroness glides into the Harlem houses,
leaves her touch on the lips
of the young blacks,
spits out your manhood with Chase
Manhattan check books—is a lover of *Negro* art.
Seaweed minutes. winter-white bleaknesses.
the icy ride of her touch up toward
the place where your penis once was.

Franks on 125th st:
        the silhouettes of our salvation
        drift rhythmically by
        as occasional strokes of laughter
        compete with the match between
        your face and hers.

For Black Writers and Artists in "Exile"

How many of them
die their deaths
between the slow rhythms and the quick,
between the going and becoming.
Time does not kill, life does, in
swift moments of hate. careless steps.
sharp glances over your shoulder.

So many of them, across dark oceans,
in smelly cafes, or along foreign banks,
or in the Countess's penthouse,
or on the avenues of speechlessness
where they have been made to
prostitute their blood
to the merchants of war that manifestly loom
behind large heads and large glasses, who
explode no myths, and who are themselves
makers of myth.

How many of them die their deaths
looking for sun, finding darkness in the city of light.
motherless, whirling in world of empty words,
snatching at, and shaping the rubbish
that is our lives
until form becomes, or life dances to an incoherent finish.

Winter 1964

Lady's Days

More song. birds follow the sun.
rain comes . . .
we drive South, me and Billie
rain.

Was it D.C.; or the hick towns
of square yokels come to hear the Lady sing?

Rain. these nights on the road, the car, these
towns lingering blue in her voice

South where birds go.
I remember them faces
the soft and the hard
faces scarred, wailing
for the song and the moan
digging the gardenia thing
she was into . . .

Lady's days

Digging the song as it turned soft
in her mouth
digging as the mouth turned softly
in the song . . .
They dug you, yeah
heavy smoke moaning
room shifting under red spotlights
And then there was the Philly bust.
Hey now lover, you said, don't worry . . .
some towns are like that . . . But the music
is somewhere else . . .

Those were copacetic times, eh Mama?
Down the hall, morning rises bright
and weird in Lester's horn.
We watch the sun scat over the river
and then our bodies merge into his song.

Lady's days

Now rain
on the road again, rain.
Herbie is driving
you sleep, pressed against my chest . . .
I can still hear Prez's solo
from last night's gig . . .
the light dreams
the warm woman in my arms
and her mellow voice hovering over us . . .
My woman
Billie beautiful
My woman, Lady Day
child of the God of Song . . .
heavy smell of alcohol and moan
spotlights for the Lady
raining gardenias and blues.

Faces. the pain rides them
more pain
their pain
ghosts ride them
your voice rides them
shifting under red spotlights . . .
smoke.

One night between sets, I asked you what it meant.
the pain raining
and the moans of scars and gardenias.
I had just finished running some scales
in quiet sixteenths when I asked you:
Is that the way it is Billie baby?
I recall you humming a line from

one of my solos
and then you laughed, that real pretty laugh.
Slow power of the blues, you said.
you said, you said that it had to go
down that way; honey, ain't gotta be no
reason for towns, faces, moans . . .

For Our Women

Out of the earth, this love
moved rivers
sang joy songs, those women wrapped
in the magic of birth
deep rivers formed your innocence
knew no evil
knew in silence
knew beyond what knowing
has come to mean
wordlessly knew.

Black women, timeless, are sun breaths
are crying mothers
are snatched rhythms
are blues rivers and food uncooked
lonely villages beside quiet streams
are agony and blood-life—fighting them back.
are sunbursts of green and yellow,
the story of the snake and the turtle
lonely roads
night rider. See-See Rider. easy men
who got lost returning to you
blues in our mother's voices
which warned us

blues people bursting out.
Like it is, I tell it;
and there are towns that
hang lonely in some man's
memory and you are there
and not there;
blacken in the soil of earth time.
Southern towns that release
their secrets to you
and then retreat, returning later
to rape.

You are there and not there.

Looming magic out of endless dreams—
our continuousness.
I see you announce their doom,
and the breath of your life
sustains us
sustains us as the sea screams out:
the female in the Middle Passage
you endured
we endured through you.

In the soul of my art, I embrace
the world that is you
as we giant-step across our earth
the sea again
again the sea unites us
as we couple with the land and the
stars of our ancestors
ancestors, stars, black universe
embrace, sky, blackness, wholeness.

1964

Abdul's Avatar and the Sun Sister's Song

For Evelyn and Yvette

Sun sperm exploding. And now, he found himself a cosmic speck bombarding through these eons, taking shape and disintegrating according to some principle that he understood that he would never ever really understand.

He bowed East in a quiet salat, thinking now that all meanings would reveal themselves to him.

But distances separated him from the beginnings. Stars also exploded somewhere over a Pleistocene landscape; winds blew eerie forms; awesome were they and without shape—blew all manner of loneliness and fear. And silences dominated that place. He knew that he had been lonely there in that time before time was marked by man. In that place, waiting for the form that was to become his body. He was the god substance. He saw himself as pre-man, the precise contours of his energy and consciousness not yet formed. Shapeless, these other strata of the mind.

O Great Father, the only God, give me strength and vision; let me not be tempted by false gods. Bodiless voice. Prayers breaking against glaciers and vague rock formations.

He waits for the Sun, and for his deliverance.

We travel the spaceways from planet to planet . . .
We travel the spaceways from planet to planet . . .
The next stop is Earth. Good old blessed green Earth, the lonely planet. Cool. Let's rest here awhile, lay ourselves in the green, and mack with the hot sun.

Then one night we came to him and showed him what fire was all about. Cool, he said, I can dig that. After the fire then comes language and tales of the fire.

*   *   *

He had been fasting for quite sometime.

He had begged to hear the voices, but Mustafa whom they said was more wise than he had forbade him from listening to them. So, although the voices came, he fought them off. He was not to hear them, but was to concentrate instead on the One true Presence which was the Presence of Almighty God, Allah. So he prayed more intently. He prayed until his body shook in frenzy; prayed so hard he ached all over and the room spun.

Well boom! The sun comes pumping light and do. Someone was in the room with him, but he couldn't make out who it was. He felt them there though. And let's speak about the light: Well it was bright and full of pain, closing his eyes tightly now, the world was a flaming red ball, membraned and twisted with dark canals. Yes. Now that my eyes were closed, I could hear the light screaming, a mad bitch. Somebody's watching me. No one had told him about this aspect of his deliverance. (I don't have to tell you that he was afraid.) Perhaps, he thought that he was in the presence of God Himself. Or perhaps, it was time for him to die. He prayed with more intensity.

But the woman would have none of that.

Aw stop all this bullshit and get some of this good pussy!

I must say that you are apparently an infidel to interrupt a man while he's praying.

I'm not trying to be nasty honey, but enough is enough. And besides, I'm tired of being ignored.

She stood there thick thighs, barefeet, a shimmering blue dress, long in length, but cut low about the breast, the dress hugging close. He felt giddy and unreal. Who are you? Nothing made sense.

Somewhere he was in a hut trembling. He could hear the beasts outside and the howls of the unholy ones reverberating through the dense foliage. Infidels, he thought. They worshipped Sun and Moon, Trees and Animals. And they believed in magic. The dress was cut low about the tits which plunged straight at his mouth.

What he wanted to say he couldn't. She was screaming with the light and changing shape from moment to moment. Times she stood before him a searing blackflame. He saw all of the stages of her life from childhood to a toothless old hag, shrunken and dry with age. Speech alternating between deep metaphysical concepts and the obscene language of a streetwalker.

And then there was the day of the boar hunt. They had tracked him toward up country. We were hot on his trail. His droppings were still fresh, we could see that. We surprised him when we came upon him suddenly. He was eating the flesh of a dead monkey. We circled as carefully as we could. Then the direction of the wind changed. It is hard to tell. But now he was haulassing it away from the gnawed monkey carcass buzzing now with flies and maggots; the scavenger birds hovered over. Kgwedi's spear caught him later in a dry rocky place where many animals go to die . . .

Don't touch me please. Like a suppressed scream. No don't, I know evil . , .

Shit. Jive ass little boy.

Then it occurred to him that perhaps he was sick and having hallucinations. After all he had been fasting. If that's the case, I'll just leave the apartment Go for a walk. See Brother Mustafa. Get me some fresh air. Yes, that would be the most righteous thing to do.

He folded up the prayer rug and placed it in a special cabinet. He wrapped the Holy Bible in soft purple velvet and put it also in its appointed place.

> Jellyroll killed my momma
> and drove my father mad . . .

Outside, he was thinking: Why did it have to go down this way? Why did his purification have to be so full of mystery and pain? Why at this moment in his life when he had cleared up so many problems did it have to be this way? Come on, tell me why? Would he ever know that? And should he ever know that? And would knowing that make him any more of a righteously spiritual person? Is this what it takes to be pure in mind and in body? Would submission to the one God, Allah, clear up these questions? There was no way of telling. But wasn't it finally a question of faith?

He would speak to Brother Mustafa about these things. Perhaps *he* would have some answers.

So I decided to discuss these things seriously with Mustafa who lived in a peaceful realm; who seemed so sure of himself and his mission in life; while I, I floundered often stumbling from thing to thing aimlessly in search of a way of life that would save me from my aimlessness, a way of life that would give me purpose and direction.

So I weaved my way through the scag freaks nodding something awful on the corners, blue dudes standing on the corner in tight clusters bartering ripped-offed goods. Walking now into the bookstore on Lenox Avenue, giving a quiet salaam to the most righteous looking sister in the place. She smiles at me and turns back to the book she is reading. Words screaming around me. Some change in the air. The day of Allah is at hand. Death to all those who do not submit. Alla-u-akbar. There was nothing worth reading here. So I depart.

Son, let me tell you about living in Georgia. Bout nineteen-twenty-four I recollect . . . In them days Negroes didn't get much schooling like you got now. We all had to go to work. Wasn't no time to be in school. Everybody making a living. But lots of us taught ourselves how to read. I had me this job with the Southern railroad. I was what they calls a pile driver . . . What's a pile driver? You mean you done been to all them schools, and read all them books, and you don't know what a pile driver is? Boy, what is they teaching you in them schools up here? Why, when I was your age, I knew about everything connected with the railroads. Boy as much as I knew, I could of run that railroad my damn self. But where was I?

You were talking about Georgia . . . But first ain't you gonna tell me what a pile driver is?

Yeah son. But right now I wanna tell you about Georgia at the time when the crackers was really crazy . . . I mean they kill a nigger no sooner than they look at him. But there was a whole lots of crazy niggers around them parts, too, and that kinda neutralized things—if you gets my meaning. Well there was this one nigger named Woody. Well, he was one crazy nigger, always cutting up on somebody. Specially on payday. Boy, he was one hardliving, hardloving, hardhitting man. He was mean, and his tongue was fast. He was always telling lies and all. Let me tell you boy . . .

Two very old black ladies were coming out of the pork store down the street from the bookstore.

They gots the best chittlins in the world in this store.

Do tell?

Yeah, I gets this new brand, put out by this new colored company in Detroit.

Do tell?

They gives you nice big slices and it's just delicious.

What they call it? I wanna get me some.

They calls it Pure Soul Chittlins.

Do declare?

Yeah, girl.

Well, I don't feel like cooking them things tonight; but I'm sure gonna try them next week. Cause my whole family likes chittlins, every now and then.

Well, Sister Johnson, it's time for me to get myself on home so I can put these things to soak. Bye, bye, see you Sunday.

She began walking up the block. She was loaded down with grocery bags. On an impulse, he asked her could he help her across the street. She looked him over quickly and thanked him graciously for offering his help. Up close, he could see that she was even older than he had thought. When the light changed green, they walked on cross the street. She spoke first.

You looks like a nice young man. Is your folks living?

Well, my mother is still alive, but my father passed away about six years ago.

Where your home?

Well, I was born in Georgia, but I grew up in Philly . . . You think you can make it now?

Well, I'd appreciate it if you would just walk me to my door; I lives above halfway down this block.

Now let me tell you about this block she lives on. The Countee Cullen Library is in that block. And here there are a great many funeral parlors. The brownstones, formerly elegant, have been chopped up into small rooms that rent for about twenty-five a week. But the most distinctive thing about this block is its small churches which usually occupy the first floor of the brownstone—there are living quarters above the church itself. You can identify some of the churches by the long awnings that stretch out over the steps. I carried her groceries to one of these.

Well this is where I live, young man.

The lettering on the tattered awning: HOLINESS CHURCH OF THE CELESTIAL MANIFESTATION—MOTHER DAB-NEY, PASTOR.

We stood under the awning.

Won't you please come in and have a cup of coffee, or something?

No ma'am, I got to be going.

Well thank you kindly for helping. By the way, my name is Mother Dabney.

My name is Abdul.

It's been nice meeting you Duel. If you ain't doing nothings on Sundays, come on by and visit your mother sometimes. After services, we have a nice meal, and it would really be a blessing to have a well-behaved young man like you to dinner.

Thank you. Thank you for the invitation. But I belong to a different religion.

Oh, that's all right. You come anyway. There's always some good people here. They're all getting old, and we need to meet young people like yourself.

Well thanks anyway, so long.

Now we were gutting the boar. We slit his throat and hung him up to drain. Then we began the long walk home where the others waited. There was plenty of meat for everyone. Around the fire, we stuffed large greasy chunks of pig into our mouths. Agwe told a tale of the sea, and we singing with all that was around us. I wanted to know my woman this night and I went to her. I touched her body there. She began to bleed. I withdrew from her. I sought out the other woman, the un-claimed one. But someone was with her. I slept alone in another place that night.

Mustafa looked out of the window on the crowded streets.

Tell me that again. You say the room was filled with light, and this woman came to you in this blinding red light while you were in the midst of your salat, my brother?

Yes, that's what happened.

I must agree. That is truly a strange thing to have happened just at that moment. It is serious, too. It is clearly symbolic of the unknowable evil that plagues our lives.

But I am not so sure of its evil nature.

It is evil, my brother. You were in the midst of your prayer, and you were tempted by a woman who you said spoke obscene language. I too have experienced such things, but that was long ago when I was a young man. And my brothers and I have often spoken of these things. If this is not a sign of evil, I don't know what is.

But she came in the light with the Eastern sun.

Shaitan has many ways of deceiving us, my brother. You were weak and tired from your labors. Therefore, it is quite understandable. You have not yet reached the righteous stage.

But what does it mean for my salvation, Brother Mustafa?

It simply means, my son, that you must reach a deeper, more penetrating level of spiritual purification. This will be difficult, but I know that you will strive harder and emerge from this test righteously. However, you must submit fully to the will of Almighty God, Allah. Right now your vibrations reek of the hog.

Why do you say that?

It is written all over your face, as the saying goes. And even though you fast, your lips are greasy with pork juice.

Brother Mustafa, I must humbly protest this kind—

You are in no position to protest anything. You are unclean still. You are still ignorant of the laws of Allah. You are still too much imbued with the spirit of the nigger. You must work harder to purge yourself of these immortal attitudes that have warped your spiritual potential and opened you up to worldly temptations. You must purge yourself of all that impedes your spiritual growth. You must purge yourself of this lingering taste for evil flesh. You must purge yourself of old habits; habits that have retarded our people for all these years under the yoke of the Beast, Shaitan, the Evil One who comes to us in many guises. Brother, with deep love in my heart for you, and with an understanding of what you are now experiencing, I must say submit to Allah, and find eternal peace.

Most honorable Mustafa, I have pledged myself to righteousness ever since before my instructions began. I have always tried to walk the correct path.

You must try harder, my son. You must try harder.

Brother Mustafa, I have done all that I can do. Is there anything else? Anything that you may have forgotten to tell me. I'm having a hard time getting this thing together. Suddenly, this woman and the voices I keep hearing—

Voices? You said nothing before about voices; what kind of voices?

I don't know. But they sound so familiar. One reminds me of my grandfather who has been dead since I was twelve years old. And then there are others too, less distinct, but felt. I suddenly feel that I am an illusion; that all of this is an illusion. There's something about a hunt and a railroad. Plus, I can almost see—

I must interrupt you, my brother. I am sorry. But I don't have much time. There is a meeting at the mosque, and I must make it. But let me take a little time to tell you this: If you want spiritual perfection, you must understand that it will be difficult. Following the righteous path is always difficult, especially for us who have lived so long in ignorance of our true selves. Come let me show you something.

He led me to the window.

We looked down on the streets. It was Saturday evening and Eldorado Cadillacs were double parked on the avenue. Niggers wearing bizarre hats and weirdly cut suits splashed in wild colors passed by laughing and fingerpopping. The dreamers and the schemers. Music was everywhere. Some woman was sleeping with another man. Sleeping around like a common slut. Some seemed steeped in an almost metaphysical loneliness. Some strutted praising their penises, snorting bowls of cheap blow, cocaine nostrils as wide as snarled boulevards. Take-off goons and bullshitting mackmen. All around Mustafa said theirs was the motion of a dead love that had to be resurrected in the one God, Allah. An old lady walked by the corner selling Martin Luther King buttons. Junkies pissed in doorways. Cop cars clicked by, slowing, scanning the streets, and the peacocking hustlers and the old folks talking about the number for the day. However, someone also played a horn somewhere.

You see, my son, this is what we, the righteous, are up against. These are the living dead. They have been made so by the Beast.

. . . So I was telling you about this bad nigger, Woody. Well, he was so bad that even the devil feared him. The white folks feared him and stayed out of that man's way. Didn't nobody mess with him less they was just as crazy as him. But bad as he was, we all liked him. He could sing and play that guitar, sho nuff, let me tell you. Only folks didn't like his singing was the church folks. They called that guitar of his a "devil box," and they didn't even want that nigger in the churchyard, let alone *in* the church. He was always singing evil songs about womens and good living, and such as that. Yeah, all us others liked him though. He didn't fear God, devil, nor man. Well, I don't have to tell you that a man like this is sure to get in trouble. Well one day, he had a run in with this cracker named Rice, and he killed that man naturally. He left town, hiding in the woods like one of them Injuns. And nobody saw him for awhile. Woody was gone, boy . . .

Goodbye, my brother. Think on these things, and Allah will surely bless you . . . By the way do you know Ibn Mirza Al-Sudan?

No, I don't think so. Why?

Perhaps you should talk to him. I understand that the brother is a Sufi. I have to split now. I will see you the same time next week?

Yeah, inshallah.

Of course, inshallah.

I leave Mustafa's resolved to be strong, to follow the path of God. There is no reason to believe that I care about you bitch. No reason at all. I will have my deliverance in spite of you, in spite of the . . .

Outside her voice buzzed his ears: I am the one who really loves you, standing here with all that I have that is godly, blessed by the worldly word. I word and world, my body your seed, your seed my body commingled together a rich swelling ocean of sperm and years. For my sufferings and the bony deaths of my children, I shit . . . Shit, I stand higher than any god you could ever hope to know, my lover. Because I am the fucking source of God . . . And dig on this lover: When you learn to love me you will be God. And if you can't get yourself together, then kiss my black ass. Embrace me screaming at you like this. Opened for you, I am. I wanna go to Kansas City where Bird and them fingerpop and play all that hip shit. I wants to parade and sashay myself around in some fine garments. I wants to devote my life to you, lover.

She broke in on him like that all the way home.

Back in his apartment now, it was quiet. He went to the cabinet where he kept his prayer rug, but it was not there. He definitely remembered putting it there (I am sure that you remember also). But perhaps, in the heat of the moment, he had unconsciously misplaced it. I looked everywhere, but I couldn't find it. Then I looked for the Koran, but it also could not be found, nor the velvet in which I had so carefully wrapped it. The room was heating up again. And I smelt incense burning.

The record machine was playing. It was 1939 and the sun was going down. His mother looks so much younger now, and he was with his father and grandfather. They were drinking corn liquor and dancing to a boogie-woogie record by Noble Sissle. He saw himself as a child sitting in a high chair, awkwardly trying to keep time with the music. His mother was doing the jitterbug. His mother was doing the jitterbug with his grandfather, the one who later in life often told him stories of the old days down home; there was the smell of hog maws and chittlins in the room stuffy with used furniture and faded draperies. Merging into that place, he is the blue haze of the poet's memory, they feel his eyes upon them, the gaze doubling, and crisscrossing back over the years. They are framed by a velvet Jesus hanging lopsided on the wall. Blue celestial manifestation pressing down on them, they slow-drag, embraced so solemn, locked into the ever so red hot holy core of the music. He watched his mother and father dancing ever so close, hugged tight there together, and singing softly along with the music, ear to ear. *O My Lover*. My grandfather sees me watching them, picks me up, and takes me to them. They stop dancing to talk to me. My mother takes me, arms full round me, brown flesh encircling this bundle of tentative energy of kicks and of ooowhs and aaahs.

Then the door was being pounded loudly. Grandfather opening it cautiously, Woody, the bad nigger, stumbling in. Said he'd escaped from down home—the crackers hot on his ass. Said he needed a place to stay for awhile. Said he had to change his name; said he was another man now. Could hear him running down something about New York. Him speaking of life now, what it's about. Gonna build something, he said. Church? School? Factory? For the colored, he said. Don't know which right now. He hugged momma. They said he was my cousin on my father's side. Then they feed him. And Woody went up to my grandfather's room and went to sleep . . .

But he couldn't find the prayer rug and his Holy Book; and the scene before him faded into the walls. Drumming now, off in the distance, rise of the green jungle sun; the woman pressing in close on him now. She pulling him toward her. The bitch in her subsiding in the voice's soft pleadings. Close now, she nibbling at his ear and rubbing kisses across his lips.

I remember the fall and the painful undertow of these years. You trying to understand me. And them mornings I wake and you not there. Soul in me aching for you, my man, lover. You and I love before love itself. Rise. Do love me honey. Please, please I know. I don't fear the circling mysteries. Take me with you. Rise, holy man. Stop gaming, move. Move with me. Move and all those years. Please rise holy man. You know I am somewhere within you always. Your God, Allah. These are only the words. The cover story. Frail names you call me by. But I am nameless; only flesh of energy. Be God and love me . . .

She pulled at him, embraced me and kissed me full in the mouth. Then she drew him to the floor where she spread herself on the prayer rug. She helped him undress, and wept as he undressed her. Quick then, he was inside of her. I was on a great sea, and I knew that I was the Sun; and I scored with my tremendous heat. And the seas parted and the ice was gone and large patches of land formed. And he was a particle of the larger explosion. And the explosion created him and he created the explosion. He had scored. And she was the place of his power; its womb and tomb. She too the explosion, the essential principle. Allah singing and scatting in him. Our song near a vague river. Everything is sure nuff everything.

Later, they bathed each other. She hummed a spiritual quietly to herself while putting on a bright red dress. She donned a yellow *gele*. I wanted to sparkle also. So I got dapped in a shimmering green suit and do. I put on some snakeskin shoes. We're gonna go to the Apollo for the soul. After the show, we gonna walk home slow up Seventh Avenue. We gonna . . . We gonna really talk to each other—you and me. And then we gonna go to bed, and talk to each other some more. We will dream like righteous lovers. But before we go to sleep we gonna thank all them voices for bringing us together. And next week, I'm gonna introduce you to Brother Mustafa. I'm sure that he would like to meet you. Since he has spoken so often of you, without really ever knowing you. And hey! I just got another idea: Since tomorrow is Sunday, we gonna go to Mother Dabney's and celebrate my deliverance. How bout that Baby? Sounds mellow to me.

The Life: Hoodoo Hollerin' Bebop Ghosts

We walked the bar
    the neon world of hip players judged us in the afterhours
    spot where they busted Booney, and where Leroy was
    blasted in the chest, in the john where we snort
    coke from tips of Broadway polished switchblades,
    talking shit, high on the ego trips.

The fly world in action
    our bitches turning Seventh Avenue tricks;
    whipping her pussy with the coat hanger,
    and saying: stop jiving bitch, get me
    the motherfuckin money now.

We walked the bar
    trying to get it together—
    ghosts of men, but men just the same.
    Yeah . . . this world judging us
    marking our progress from cradle
    to cane, laughing, wishing us luck
    while we hover over pits of dry bones
    laughing like forgotten pimps—we so hip.

It's all here
    all down here in the neon world of flash
    and-let-me-fuck-you bullshit.

Even in our weakness here, somewhere we are strong some
snake–skinned god hisses here:
    hoodoo hollerin' bebop ghosts
    some eternal demon squirming
    in his head—that's why he be bad
    and all them things.

Some of us
    teetered on the edge of the Life like peeping
    toms; teetered maneuvering for the grand score
    that came every night, but every night, came late.
        dope pushers
        take-off goons
        Murphy-working old ladies
    one used to dance in the high yaller chorus
    of the Cotton Club;
    one, a nympho, claimed once to have graduated
    from Vassar. (If you can dig it?)
    Scenes like that were quite common.

One, a singer, a Chanel No. 5 freak from South Philly called
herself the Duchess, spoke with an English accent.
                        Lois
    the envious one, frail hunk of bones
    and cigarette holder, wraps spider legs around dull
    honky sailors; likes going down on Market Street
    cowboys.

Up under it all
some ancient memory trying to break through the
perpetual high:
He be hoodoo hollerin' bebop ghosts
some awesome demon twisting close
curling in the smell of beer
and reefer; some dick strong god
hissing softly in his ear
        Hey!
And he is mean with his nigger rod
thus note the smell of sen-sen on his breath
but dig how he teeters on the edge of death . . .

Spring 1969

Scag Dream

Clouds   I saw
        rose   to greet them
        I   twisted my eyes
            shaping fables
from eerie forms   I
        wanted to see   ghosts
        saw them   I wanted to die   and
        I died

1971

Ghost Poem #1

You would never shoot smack
or lay in one of these Harlem
doorways pissing on yourself
that is not your way   not the
way of Alabama boys groomed slick
for these wicked cities momma
warned us of

You were always swifter than that:
the fast money was the Murphy game
or the main supply before the cutting—
so now you lean with the shadows
(at the dark end of Turk's bar)
aware that the hitman is on your ass

You know that there is something inevitable
about it
You know that he will come   as sure as shit
snorting blow for courage
and he will burn you at the peak of your peacocking
glory
And when momma gets the news
she will shudder over the evening meal
and moan: "Is that my Junie Boy runnin
with that fast crowd?"

Winter 1971

Can I Tell You This Story, or Will You Send Me through All Kinds of Changes?

> *Summer city,*
> *asphalt memory*
> *of blood and pain,*
> *night game*
> *the eerie rain;*
> *we had no pity*
> *on the weak ones . . .*
>
> —Charles Neal

Stiff old Philly saints dripped gold into the arms of Georgia Queens; Columbia Avenue was snake eyes and the hussy in red.

In those days, the avenues were nigger cops, like Reedy who thought he was the Durango Kid; we shot him in the doorway of a mean loud party.

These were the days of the bebopping house of blue lights.

Bird gained weight; we meet our turnpike death clutching our instruments.

Places got turned out then—
heads were busted and lips swelled purple;
we were blind.
we stayed high on Mexicano marijuana,
drank wine in narrow alleys,
and Lady Melody, the blue spirit breezed
in every now and then.

We were killed in weird ways,
puked guts, stabbed heads, bleeding marcels,
cursing each other's mothers and fathers and sisters and
brothers;
old dribble-lipped drunks high on tokay spewing and pissin
on themselves.
And Daddy Grace mad with power, shoving pigfeet and barbecue
down the throats of shouting soul sisters.
Preachers dreamed yellow Cadillacs,
waiters pretending doctor,
mailmen pretending lawyer,
doctor and lawyer pretending Negro society.

These were the Eisenhower years—the landscape of the fifties.
                    The whole thing was a skunky bitch,
legs in a putrid spread, obscene these Northern cities.
                    And no prophets walked these streets;
                    or at least, we did not know them.

Can I tell this story?
We slow-dragged, our do-rags wrapped, like Harlem sheiks,
a thin swish of sweat darkening
the edge of silk scarfs.

Horns on bats' wings hollered high,
the saxes seemed to carry the deepest tales;
and even the smells had meaning.
our rhythms played stink finger with the moon.
we died bullshit deaths
behind urinating staircases.

                    High yallers moved to Germantown;
and Summer saw an invasion of Southern dark brown chippies.
                    Each king's reign ended in the
slick slash of air-teasing razors.
                    But boiling lye was the weapon
of lonely plump old maids.
We formed nations, and bopped all over the city, gang-warring.
we were blind then, and even now the light is hard to take.
For some the winters were blue lights, the slow grind,

Johnny Ace dying of Russian roulette, cocaine, and the hawkeyed, the hawkeyed wind tearing at our asses; home was candy
stores, stuffy rooms, the burning incense of shattered bebop
poets who had seen Bird and wanted to be Bird in all the
ways that Bird was.

So they spread their asses
for the Scag God to fuck them;
and so, some nights they sat high
in the Diamond Street cemetery
talking to Yoruba ghosts.
It was not our time or place;
it was an empty time,
an asphalt bridge stretching into nowhere
some words
some deaths
somebody pinned
against the wall
gun up under his throat.

                        And all we wanted
                        to do was sing like *moonglow*
                        ravens or raspy-voiced old
                        blues singers. times we wanted
                        to be killers slouching treacherous
                        under broad skies.

So we twisted our dreams and shaped
our worlds out of lean fables
and awesome toasts that sucked
us into streams of moody anger—
to turn our lips down and be
angry was at the pit of the style.

                        So, we danced, switchblades nestled
                        in socks or back pockets
                        as we   as we   as we glide
                        under the mystic aura
                        of black Buddhas and voodoo gods

Whole chunks of life lay chopped up in alleys—
fresh-born babies wrapped in the classified
pages of the *Philadelphia Tribune*;
in our boredom, we allowed streetwalkers
to seduce us while the smells from fish n' chips
drifted into two-room apartments adorned
with velvet Jesuses.

God bless this house of body and of desperation
of blood and of story of gesture and of nighttime hassles.

We died and killed for our puny reps:
"Shove that punk in his chest, break his
head, blast that motherfucker," sez Camel
Hair Benny, the no-tooth killer.

Spring was loose, the surge of color
                    the park
                    and her body
                    as holy object,
                    walks along
                    the Schuylkill.
                    love hard today
                    cause death
                    rules the avenues
                    as do
                    rhythm and change
                    kiss
                    under the Japanese gazebo
                    kiss
                    smells, soft plunge
                    wet joy and all
                    moans and the clutching fingers
                    screams
                    tears when you first split her.

It was not hard to be tender when
the heart like wide boulevards lay exposed
for the shuffling armies and the demon preachers
who would soon descend upon us flailing whips,

cursing, teaching submission to a bullshit god.
Parents and uncles would join the act, too;
the whore aunt would argue the virtues
of virginity, fat and high on beer, sucking reefer.
Their nights would end in spilled wine
and the lonely odor of cigarette butts—
their curses would greet the sun;
but most of our spring nights would end
in mellow morning songs and soft rain . . .

1970

Malcolm X—An Autobiography

I am the Seventh Son of the son
who was also the seventh.
I have drunk deep of the waters of my ancestors,
have traveled the soul's journey toward cosmic harmony—
the Seventh Son.

Have walked slick avenues
and seen grown men, fall, to die in a blue doom
of death and ancestral agony;
have seen old men glide, shadowless, feet barely
touching the pavements.

I sprang out of the Midwestern plains
the bleak Michigan landscape, the black blues of Kansas
City, these kiss-me-nights;
out of the bleak Michigan landscape wearing the slave name
Malcolm Little.

Saw a brief vision in Lansing when I was seven, and in
my momma's womb heard the beast cry death;

a landscape on which white robed figures ride, and my
Garvey father silhouetted against the night-fire
gun in hand,
form outlined against a panorama of violence.

Out of the Midwestern bleakness, I sprang, pushed eastward,
past shack on country nigger shack, across the wilderness
of North America.
I hustler. I pimp. I unfulfilled black man
bursting with destiny.
New York City Slim called me Big Red,
and there was no escape, close nights of the smell of death.
Pimp. Hustler. The day fills these rooms.
I'm talking about New York, Harlem.
Talking about the neon madness.
Talking about ghetto eyes and nights
Talking about death protruding across the room
Talking about Small's Paradise.
Talking about cigarette butts, and rooms smelly with white
sex-flesh, and dank sheets, and being on the run.
Talking about cocaine illusions.
Talking about stealing and selling.
Talking about these New York cops who smell
of blood and money.
I am Big Red, tiger, vicious, Big Red, bad nigger, will kill.

But there is rhythm here
Its own special substance:
I hear Billie sing, no Good Man, and dig Prez, wearing
the Zoot suit of life, the Porkpie hat tilted at the
correct angle; through the Harlem smoke of beer and
whiskey, I understand the mystery of the Signifying
Monkey;
in a blue haze of inspiration
I reach for the totality of being.
I am at the center of a swirl of events.
War and death.
Rhythm.
Hot women.
I think life a commodity bargained

for across the bar in Small's.
I perceive the echoes of Bird
and there is a gnawing the maw
of my emotions.

And then there is jail.
America is the world's greatest jailer,
and we are all in jails
Holy spirits contained like magnificent
birds of wonder.
I now understand my father urged on by the ghost of Garvey,
and see a small brown man standing in a corner.
The cell. Cold. Dank.
The light around him vibrates.
(Am I crazy?)
But to understand is to submit to a more perfect will,
a more perfect order.
To understand is to surrender the imperfect self
for a more perfect self.

Allah formed man, I follow
and shake within the very depth of my most interesting being;
and I bear witness to the Message of Allah
and I bear witness; all praise is due Allah.

Spring 1967

The Summer after Malcolm

The Summer after Malcolm, I lost myself in a jet stream of mad
words, acts, goading bits of love memory. Like that. It was a
cold bitch. I mean the pain. Dig, all summer long, I could see
Malcolm's face drifting with the sound of Harlem children. Old
men played checkers on the blocks running between Seventh

and Eighth. And yes, there was a moan in the sweating night. The wine smells and hallways were screaming women. Angry the way the breeze came off from the river. Angered, too, by the rustle of soft murmuring silhouettes in the dark park. Child of demon lover, I grappled with ancestral ghosts. It was Smokey Robinson's summer, the hip falsetto, the long lean lover.

Missed you baby. Missed her smell and awkwardness, the brown walk, soft spots in the dark of her. Night turns on its edges. Dig, it was a still clinging that robbed sleep those summer nights.

Remember baby. Under the beat, music spiraling over us, under the beat, and O how we clung and took that lovely, lovely, very mellow, super special ride?

But that Summer after Malcolm marks my phase in time. After Malcolm, the seasons turned stale. There was a dullness in the air for awhile. And you had gone, and there was a lingering beauty in the pain. Now there are scraps of you here and there in the backwash of my mind. And check this: lurking between odd pages in a book of blues, your handwriting in red ink . . .

1966/1973

Love Song in Middle Passage

We plunge through time
and feel
the westward pull of death—
slave ships flank the shore,
across the veldt, songs,
moaning spirits and lonely rhythms;
voices plunge, screaming blood.

in time's body
as
slick white knives slit back throats,
chew black brains, tearing their bodies
piece by piece, flesh-eating pirates.
and even though we be life itself
we must kill.

Sea-winds moan, one, Fulani warrior, breaks
a slave-runner's skull,
then kills his black self rather
than never see his land or children,
or hear the spirits of his ancestors
moving in the vibrations of the drum.

and even though we be life itself
we must kill.
must will death to white sea monsters
and their pale shit smelling philosophies.

Red glow of sea-death mornings.
and where will it end?
and who will end it?
our summits are endless
deep within
the soil-cosmos of our spirits.

and even though we be life
we must kill,
gouging out pale sea-water eyes,
crushing them and their generations,
spitting destruction upon their cities
which burn like plastic dreams;
blacks boogaloo through their cities shouting
and burning, hurling precise death-curses,
stone-cold killers bursting with revenge.
break through.
breaking through their time into our own.

even though we are the sun's song,
the roar, the surge, the rhythm and poetry;

the shocked sounds of saxophones, old men,
dancing children, and the women singing funky blues,
we must destroy
to live.

On the Sea's horizon McNamara scientists
with Ph D's
lurk
twist bomb dials, manipulate Negro organizations.
contrive CIA chaos, while drinking Emmett Till's
blood. (Welcome to Mississippi

       land of sweet magnolias.)

We must become stone-cold killers,
panther-spirits, invisible men,
night specters: your uncle tom teeth brightly grin
or you scratch your stepin' fetchit head,
while thrusting the blade into the beast-heart,
and still grinning with your uncle tom grin,
say: "you de boss, boss, heh, heh, heh, heh,
      now try this for size, motherfucker!"

then expand,
sucking in the meaning of your discovery,
sucking in the liberated wonder of the cosmos,
expanding until the world is filled with
a vibrating black light.

It's the Year of the Snake
1965

It's the year of the snake,
he slips wisely through
oppressive weeds;
the foliage of the beast grows
in rough tumbles toward
the sky of their destruction,
bureaucratic tombs release
CIA agents
with tin cups and dark glasses;
and
taxi-cab drivers with poison
in their eyes
shoot toward Harlem.
pop up in Congo
sporting death in black
embassies.

The snake protects himself,
sees madness
in their stares,
as artful murderers
appear in the Audubon of our hope
as the Merchants of War
sparkle with a demonic brilliance
and
the Negro professor betrays his children
as
he breeds wooden freaks
under the wings of the Eagle's
dripping talons.

In the year of the snake
we are warned:
beware of the mark of the Beast,
death to those who bear it.

Rizzo's Nightmare

Sees niggers turning in his sleep,
has visions of his wife being fucked
by big black brothers with wooly hair;
Rizzo otherwise known as Cisco Kid hates the real black
who would kick his nightmare in the teeth,
turning his pale bitch out into the cold north
where she really belongs.

Rizzo sees niggers turning his snowbound dreams,
hates color, hates swirling agadadasm and rhythm
he can not make, but would destroy the rhythm
of the spiritual world; would have you pale
and full of self-doubt, a stumbling fool from
washington lane, or a weak-voiced tom on Mayor Tate's
Urban Coalition.
Rizzo otherwise known as the Cisco Kid dreams himself
a mussolini destroying the Ethiopian night,
pushed to the wall we will return, burning and cutting,
and in the eye of the thing, we will find Rizzo
and murder him, stripping him naked to the black
light of truth, execute him and mount his head
on a stake in city hall court yard.

Brother Pimp

In memory of Iceberg Slim and others
who have walked these streets

Brother Pimp, you ain't shit;
and neither are we without you.
I used to dig your hip ways,
but you ain't shit yet;
and neither are we without you.
you just as bad as the honky,
only you dress better motherfucker,
only you drive your cadillac better mother-
fuck-er.

You help the beast make whores out of black women,
only you yourself are a whore.
you and your brother pimps kill each other
for the right to destroy our women.
would-be heroes. would-be black men.

JOIN THE STRUGGLE
FOR REAL MANHOOD
LINK YOUR NATURAL LIFE-SENSE
TO THE REAL SOUL-THING

become a new kind of pimp. yeah, brother, pimp for the
revolution. I say pimp for the revolution,
not pimp on the revolution.
brother, would-be hero. would-be black man,
a man does not allow his women to go down
on sick white beasts,
to kill the soul for the shit green of dead beasts,
to kill the soul and call it hip;
yeah, motherfucker, you ain't shit.

you just another kind of slave master,
only you black, man, and that really ain't cool.

I'm hip to you chump, and don't run no game
about the honky's money;
until you join the black thing
                you are suspect.
until you join the black thing
                you are enemy.
until you join the black thing

Kuntu

I am descended from Drum
I am descended from Drum
from that which first formed
from that which first formed
descended from Drum.
the first that formed
the first that formed
I am from the first that formed
the pulse that formed
the pulse that formed
the pulse that formed the Word
the pulse that formed the Word
and the Word informing the Universe
and the Word informing the Universe
and the Word informing the pulse
Word and pulse and Universe
Word and pulse and Universe.
the first that formed to link
to link Word and act
to link Word and substance
to link Word and desire

2

Word, act, and Universe
the first form out of the Earth
Drum's Earth and Black Earth faces
Drum's Song and Black Earth song
　　　first Song in the black of Olorun
in Olorun, the Universe, I formed
the Word and the Earth and linked
them in the dance
the first form was formless sound
the first Word was Drum's Word
I am descended from Drum
Drum's words informed us, giving us flesh
and flesh shaped the Word.
I say, and flesh shaped the Word
linked the song
linked Earth to sky

3

No wonder, we float so lightly
these summer night songs in us
we float, bopping high on the rhythms of Drum;
do air-dances O so lightly,
powered by the informing Drum,
the all-slithering hiss
of eternal God-substance,
here form curls serpentine
ropes of bull-churned stars
and my Mighty Father
the heart of it all.

Drum song there: Cinque, Amistad, Watts.
Drum song there: Vassa, Massa, Jamestown.
Drum song there.
Drum song there: Harriet, chariot, broken circles.
Drum song there: flames, these cities, our time.

1966

About the Author

Lawrence P. Neal was born in 1937 in Atlanta, Georgia. He was co-founder of the Black Arts Repertory Theater in Harlem and was one of the editors of *Black Fire: An Anthology of Afro-American Writing*, a seminal anthology of the Black Arts Movement. During his life he served as executive director of the Commission on the Arts and Humanities in Washington, D.C., and as an instructor at a number of institutions, including the City College of New York, and Howard and Yale Universities. He also served as education director of the Panther Party. In 1971 he received a Guggenheim Fellowship. He died in Hamilton, New York in 1981.